CONSENSUALITY

Navigating Feminism, Gender, and Boundaries Towards Loving Relationships

Helen Wildfell

Consensuality: Navigating Feminism, Gender, and Boundaries Towards Loving Relationships
Helen Wildfell

First Printing, July 14, 2015
All text is © Helen Wildfell

This edition is © Microcosm Publishing, 2015
Design and illustration by Meggyn Pomerleau
Edited by Taylor Hurley
The typeface used in this book is SmytheSans,
designed by Ian Lynam

For a catalog, write
Microcosm Publishing
2752 N. Williams Ave
Portland, OR 97227
or visit MicrocosmPublishing.com

ISBN 978-1-62106-004-8
This is Microcosm #192

Distributed worldwide by Legato / Perseus and in the
UK by Turnaround.

This book was printed on post-consumer paper in the U.S.

FOREWORD

There are infinite possibilities in human relationships,

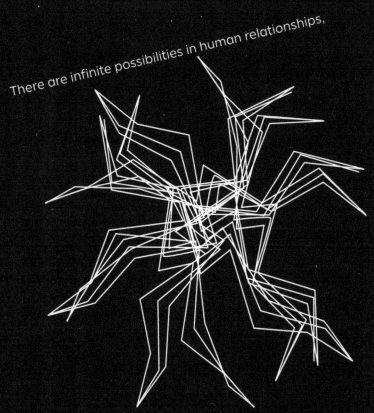

but the fairytale ideal of companionship does not exist for most people.

Creating happy, consensual relationships is a complicated endeavor. When you care about people, you are forming a complex bond that develops through layers of varying perspectives and boundaries.

In order to build healthy relationships, it is important to recognize that we all view the world through a subjective lens. I intentionally use a personal tone throughout *Consensuality* to reveal that I am a subjective individual. I am a white, heterosexual ciswoman, and the reality is that my perspective causes me to focus on particular issues. I emphasize how gender and sexual interactions affect my emotions and personal relationships. It is very likely, however, that someone with a different background (or even a similar one) could find an alternative approach to gender and sexuality.

All people should have an equal right to express their own form of feminism, so I do not want *Consensuality* to contribute to the false impression that white ciswomen can represent all women. It would be unfair to assume that my voice could somehow create a universal guide to feminist relationships. I imagine that most people primarily discover personal boundaries through their own experiences of feeling trespassed or rewarded with consent. And I hope that you as the reader will consider your own identity as you read the book.

Before beginning your journey into *Consensuality*, examine your perspective. Explore

what you need from yourself and others. Really dig deep. It is time to go far beyond what you want in a partner. Explore who you are right now and what you want for yourself. You may come from a privileged background, or you may have been subjected to many injustices. You may value independence, or perhaps you are looking for additional support.

Ask yourself now:

> How do you see yourself?
> What is your view of gender and sexuality?
> How does this affect your relationships?
> Do you feel comfortable in your current relationships?
> Where is your starting point in this journey?

Consensuality will act as your companion as you navigate through feminism, gender, and sexual boundaries. It includes exercises that provide a space for you to process your feelings. The book will not cover every issue you encounter, but it should empower you to express yourself in all of your interactions. Romantic or not, a supportive friend will listen to your perspective, and in return, you should encourage them to express their views as well.

Listening to one another will hopefully evolve into caring for one another. Respectful communication is essential. If you are healing from an abusive past, explore bonds with people who show consideration for your perspective. On the other hand, if you have abused another person, be aware of how you can avoid hurting friends and partners in the future. You may have been on both sides of abuse. In that case, *Consensuality* can provide a path towards untangling the complex reactions of mutually dysfunctional relationships. If you continually disagree with a significant other, through this process, you may find that you two are not a good match for a close relationship. When a person truly respects your perspective, they will feel empathy for you even if your viewpoints differ.

Names have been removed or changed to protect everyone described in this book. Continue the consideration by taking care of yourself and others while reading through these pages. *Consensuality* contains perspectives on many issues that require collaboration to properly process, including sexual assault, substance abuse, and emotional dysfunction. Go slow, and don't hesitate to stop and reflect. Consider how your relationships with friends, family, lovers, and co-adventurers relate to the personal experiences in the book. Discover your *Consensuality.*

INTRODUCTION

PART 1

REGRETFUL **15**

RESENTFUL **40**

RESPECTFUL **59**

PART 2

A GLOSSARY

10

15

90

124

INTRODUCTION

For a long time, I tried to deal logically with my relationship issues. I would jot down any psychological damage in need of repair as if I was compiling a "honey-do" list:

- My compulsive need to always say "sorry"
- My inability to be assertive
- My lack of control
- My resentment towards men
- My fear of rape
- My association of sex with rape

Lists like the one above showed how easy it was for me to feel bad about myself. They were a simple way to recognize issues without fully understanding where they came from. Although my concerns were legitimate, I was not learning how to resolve them in my relationships. My frustrations remained hidden until my inability to express these feelings oozed into my daily life.

At age twenty-one, after years of denying my feelings, I moved into a dilapidated campus apartment where the level of respect was dismal. A poor, neglected guinea pig squeaked in the living room corner, while my roommate and her boyfriend screamed at each other daily. I had no idea how to handle my new environment, but I was attempting to build some sense of self-respect.

It was my first time living without a parent or a significant other. I had a boyfriend, but I had moved out of his house in order to "find myself." He could act like a parent at times. Certain food, cigarettes, and other items that he saw as hazardous had been restricted under his roof. In addition, I felt indebted to him because I had never paid rent at his house.

So to celebrate my independence in my apartment, I planned to go out with two of my best friends. It seemed like a normal thing for a 21-year-old to do. I told my boyfriend that I was going to spend time with my friends that night. I did not expect to see him.

But my nights out with friends were always a source of concern for my boyfriend. He had a different agenda. He suggested to my friends that we pick him up and go to a bar closer to his house. I only found out about his idea when my friends were on their way to my apartment. I didn't want to create drama, so I accepted the change in plans.

When we met with him, he was already intoxicated, which immediately filled me with anger. When my boyfriend and I drank together, things often went horribly wrong. We began the turbulent night by arguing without resolution. I struggled to hold back

my resentment, but after only five minutes, I needed to get away from him.

I asked my friends if they wanted to walk to get some food, thinking I could temporarily avoid further conflict. I was unaware that, according to my boyfriend, we would be wandering around a bad neighborhood. He snapped at me:

"Yeah, why don't you just go and get raped."

Upon hearing the statement, years of shame broke out of me and *I slapped him as hard as I could.*

Silence followed; neither of us could emotionally process what had happened. I had felt a similar level of rage in previous fights with him, but I was always able to control my emotions. At worst, I would strangle my frustration by screaming into a pillow. Now, all I knew was that my boyfriend had verbally crossed my boundaries and I had hit him in response.

Later that night, delayed reactions continued to pour out of our bruised psyches. His frustrations leaked into further damage, which ended with him yelling at me for being "fucking stupid." I was tired of his **verbal abuse**; I finally saw our destructive potential realized in these moments. He had previously admitted to me that he had also slapped an ex-girlfriend, but before the night I hit him, I had denied our anger towards each other.

My friends rushed me out of the situation when I broke into tears of frustration. They took me somewhere I would feel safe, my apartment, where we talked for hours about the complications of my relationship. They showed me that there were people who respected my thoughts and feelings, even if I didn't know how to respect myself. I felt very small and ashamed in this moment. I had stayed in this verbally abusive relationship for years as my self-esteem deteriorated. Most disappointing to me was that I had now physically abused him. My boyfriend showed up with flowers and chocolates on my doorstep the next day. Noticing the gifts, my roommate even remarked how I must have a sweet boyfriend. But presents could not explain how to stop hurting each other, nor could they undo the emotional damage that had already been done. The alcohol erased his memories of the night, and I stored the information for ammo in future fights. Neither one of us was properly equipped to maintain a healthy relationship.

People told me that it wasn't a big deal to slap a man, and when I heard other stories about men in drunken mishaps, "boys will be boys" was a common explanation. It was easy to lean on gender stereotypes when they allowed us to justify our actions. The whole situation could be normalized, from the hurtful things he said to the **physical abuse** I inflicted.

> → *What qualities about this person make them a good partner?*
> • *What things irritate or upset you?*
> • *Can you identity why your partner might behave this way?*
> • *Can you look past these traits?*

So what could I do?

It wasn't as simple as getting out of the relationship, which felt nearly impossible. Self-esteem issues ate at both of us. Insecurities kept me within the confines of the relationship, isolated from others. On the other hand, his fears seemed to be expressed through alcohol use and attempts to control his surroundings. I often attributed our problems to his excessive drinking, but distrust also developed when he encouraged me to drink. In between sober affection, drunken sex was normal for us. Unwanted sex was normal for me. The emotions of our dysfunctional relationship were cyclical, pushing and pulling away from each other. We had been in the cycle for so long, it felt natural to go back and forth between anger and love.

As a result of our duplicitous bond, the relationship lasted much longer than it should have. It only ended after I found the tools to care of myself, and even then, there was regret to deal with after the break-up. I needed to examine everything I knew about myself if I hoped to create healthy relationships in the future. I had to understand the sources of my shame and resentment before I could discover confidence. This meant exploring the internal problems I had shelved away my whole life, spanning from issues with my family, the way I was raised, and the way I viewed gender roles in relation to myself. The night I hit my boyfriend, I began a complex search for something that I couldn't understand yet—*consensuality*.

PART I: HEALING THROUGH FEELINGS

REGRETFUL

Professional counseling was the first tool I used to explore my feelings about that night. I wanted to understand how I had arrived at this point. I wanted to examine why I regretted so many of my actions and feelings. Because I had grown up with the belief that there was some sort of cosmic balance to traditional gender roles, an idea that I had inherited from my dad, I was struggling with how I could be assertive as a female without being violent.

Now involved in a dysfunctional relationship and seeing that my previous notions of gender weren't working, I turned on the person who taught me about the social divide between male and female. In and out of counseling appointments, I complained about my dad often and wondered why I couldn't get over my issues. With good intentions, counselors often tried to remind me that my dad didn't have a manual for

raising me, but all I could see was that my dad and society hadn't given me the right guide for my life.

Growing up, I lived with regret and confusion over my decisions. I was praised for bending to others' wills, rather than holding to my own beliefs. Instead of confronting my issues, I learned to navigate around them. My father would tell me that I was a "master of feminine energy," so it was ingrained in me that I was somehow a better person for fitting into the stereotypical gender role. I didn't try to expand outside of that identity because I didn't know there were other options. Instead, I felt regret, without the means to understand why.

Regret was an unwanted tool that I didn't know how to use. I could rationalize how I had made a mistake in order to passively learn from it, but I didn't understand that there were alternative routes. More often than not, regret continued when I failed to adjust my actions. It went like this: "Why didn't I say that?" or "Why didn't I act before it was too late?" or "Why didn't I stand up for myself?" Always the "Why didn't I?" Never the "Why did I?" The ultimate passive person: I did not do what I wanted to do and I almost always regretted it.

My mom and dad were self-proclaimed hippies. They watched as second wave feminism emerged, witnessing

LIFE IS EASIER WITHOUT GENDER ROLES

the major changes in birth control and reproductive rights. They were liberal and open-minded when it came to religion, health, and many social issues, but something was left behind. Even if my dad was comfortable with external social change, he still believed that women and men should have different roles in personal relationships. Masculine equaled aggressive and feminine equaled passive in his mind.

My dad felt comfortable exposing his beliefs by criticizing women that didn't fit into his definition of feminine. In particular, he judged my sister and mother for having strong, outgoing personalities. Learning from his reactions to my female family members, I knew what would make me look better in his eyes, but I didn't realize that I could question his views as well. I didn't understand that being socialized into a particular role could negatively affect my future relationships.

Up until age eighteen, I had little understanding of any form of feminism. My mom taught me the importance of a woman's right to reproductive health, but I had no idea how this was related to the larger social issue of gender inequality. Before I went to college, I didn't have access to comprehensive education on any type of social justice. I struggled to grasp how gender inequality affected my relationships. It took years of nudging through dysfunctional relationships for me to realize that the concept of patriarchy in our society allowed many men to justify their dominant role in personal relationships.

When I finally told my dad that my wants didn't fit into his idea of traditional gender roles, he still disagreed with me. He was adamant that most people innately fulfilled his gendered descriptions, but he accepted that I wanted something different. For the first time, I had expressed my opinion to my dad instead of absorbing his ideals. The experience empowered me to move forward with new relationships in my own way.

I'm Sorry For Doubting Myself

"Sorry" was my favorite word for a long time. The first time I had a feminist counselor she helped me understand why I felt the need to say that I was sorry after every other sentence. She helped me understand why I felt regret so often. She explained how, unfortunately, "sorry" can be viewed as a "feminine" word.

A 2010 study on apology differences between men and women found that female participants were more likely to report committing offenses against other people. The sample population, which consisted only of Canadian college students, limited the study. Still, the findings eerily match my personal experience and the common opinion that women apologize more than men [1].

---

1 Schumann, K., & Ross, M. *Why Women Apologize More Than Men: Gender Differences In Thresholds For Perceiving Offensive Behavior.* Psychological Science, 21(11), 1649-1655.

"Sorry" is meant to express regret for something said or done, but I found myself saying it even when I didn't have a reason for regret. I accepted guilt for everything at the first sign of social discomfort. "Sorry" slashed through many of my opinions and feelings, often counteracting my justifiable emotional responses. I realized that "sorry" wasn't just a word, it was sculpting my identity. It was affecting how I felt about myself.

In the "About Me" section of a previous online profile, I dutifully accepted my fate by listing, "Sometimes I'm confused, usually I don't know, but most of the time I'm just sorry." It seemed silly when I wrote it because I was aware that I overused the word. I had been taught that being female meant navigating around conflict at the expense of my own feelings. Being "sorry" was the easiest way for me to dissolve disagreements. If I apologized enough, I thought I could move on. In reality, I was holding onto more and more resentment.

After I would say "sorry", people usually responded with, "It's ok." They accepted my guilt and we moved forward, but our relationship then developed an unequal power dynamic. My emotions did not seem to matter as much as theirs. Although I could express myself in private, sometimes in destructive ways, my feelings were often ignored in my relationships. I needed to rewire how I approached my relationships, and my loved ones needed to respect my opinions in our interactions.

My Destructive Behaviors

1. Saying "Sorry" Without Doing Anything Wrong

Relationships are hard. If you're like me, you may have an even harder time dealing with the complex emotions that arise in social interactions. Maybe you've hurt yourself or know someone else dealing with self-harm. If these behaviors sound familiar, explore professional programs, such as mental health resources and/or gender equality centers, that can provide additional means for coping.

As my most common destructive behavior, the damage of saying "sorry" came from the misuse and abundance of the word in my vocabulary. If I had to guess, I probably used this word up to fifty times a day. I used it for everything—my job, my home life, my sex life, etc. The use of "sorry" with regards to sex, in particular, wreaked havoc on my self-esteem. If I didn't want to have sex when someone proposed the idea to me, I would always say "sorry". Sometimes I still say "sorry" when I don't want to have sex and my partner does. Thankfully, I've communicated my tendency towards guilt to my current partner and he does not consider my apology as an admission of wrong-doing. Even when my socialized vocabulary says otherwise, he understands that I have control over my own body.

2. Drinking Excessively

My ex-boyfriend would drink every day, so prior to the break-up, I saw excessive drinking as his destructive behavior. As mentioned earlier, drinking seemed to mask his self-esteem issues. But shortly after ending the relationship, I began making frequent trips to my favorite bar. If I had a free night, I was destined to end up there. Unintentionally, I gradually increased the amount of drinks I had in a night. Even if I had work the next day, the need to drink seemed too hard to resist. Drinking itself wasn't necessarily an issue, but how I used the drinking became a problem. After about six months of bar-hopping, I realized that I was using alcohol as a coping mechanism.

3. Physical Self-Harm

The least apparent of all of my destructive behaviors was the most damaging—physical self-harm. I had begun scratching myself when I was 13 years old. At that age, I thought women were more likable when they were passive, so my family and friends generally did not know when I was upset. Instead of approaching people for help, I mistakenly thought it was admirable to quietly hurt myself. Even into adulthood, when I legally had more control over my own decisions, the habit of physically harming myself continued. It became one of the few ways I knew of expressing extreme negative emotion.

When I moved across the country to Virginia for a semester of school, no one knew that I had developed the extremely destructive habit of self-harm. So when a bout of my homesickness spiraled out of control, everyone was surprised by my intentional overdose on painkillers. I was even surprised, as I had tricked myself into believing that my habit was under control. Thankfully, in the shock of my depression, I didn't hide the overdose. I called my mom, who contacted the campus police. I was taken to the hospital and treated.

The experience exposed my family to the emotions I had been suppressing. Over the next several years, I received more support from my family, but my personal recovery was slow and intermittent. Though rare, there were still moments that I resorted to cutting or scratching myself to express grief. Unfortunately, I believe I will always feel some urge to hurt myself in moments of depression, but I also know that destructive behaviors can be prevented and healed with positive interactions. Thus far, forming communicative relationships has been the greatest coping mechanism for combating self-harm.

Going Beyond Destructive Behaviors and Learning to Live (Feel) in All Moments

I always treated "living in the moment" as some alternate reality that I would never experience. I thought my brain wasn't wired to live in that reality. I was lingering in regret instead. Destructive behaviors often restricted my self-expression to private and painful moments.

Like a hose with a kink in it, emotions flowed through me, but only a trickle would come out. Some people preferred for me to be passive. My feelings or wants would rarely inconvenience people, but kept inside, my feelings and wants also couldn't help anyone. They didn't help me understand myself; they didn't help others understand me. Without regular expression of my emotions, my view of the world was very limited. I over-valued restraint and saw others' emotional reactions as a weakness. Out of fear that my own feelings might be exposed, I avoided interactions with other people who I perceived as emotional.

As a result, my feelings became so restricted that it was painful. I would get depressed or angry when the unexpressed emotions would boil over. I would go to counseling, but it was very difficult to begin allowing more emotions out in my everyday life. I associated the release of feelings with extreme moments of depression, such as when I overdosed on painkillers. I felt guilty if I let more than a trickle out.

I wasn't able to accept my feelings until it became more apparent that resentment and guilt were

interfering with the positive relationships in my life. After a series of dysfunctional relationships, I became pickier about who I allowed in my life. I worked hard to only continue relationships with people who respected me, but I still had trouble finding respect for myself.

When I began dating my current partner, I felt extreme anxiety if he showed dissatisfaction or simply left to go home for the night. I couldn't understand why I was co-dependent and I tried to ignore these feelings, but they would culminate into a panic attack. The condensed anxiety lasted a few minutes, during which my brain flooded with fear. I felt as if I was going to die; my past regrets were doing all they could to push everything away. I couldn't continue to live with unwarranted guilt.

Bursting with a need for outward expression, one of the first things I did was shave part of my head—something I'd wanted to do for years but had been afraid of what people's reactions would be. My physical appearance became an important form of expression in my repressed emotional state. I was learning to display my physical appearance how I wanted to, regardless of awkward stares and comments. It was the beginning of my realization that I had a right to express myself.

The next part of changing how I viewed my personality and emotions was much longer and more significant. I started expressing my inner feelings. I openly told others that I apologized too much. I noticed and removed many of the unnecessary disclaimers usually included in my speech. For example, I often prefaced my statements with, "you're going to hate me for this," so I did my best to remove the phrase from my vocabulary. Small decisions, like choosing a restaurant where a friend and I could eat, became moments of empowerment. I shared what I wanted in big and little ways. After holding in my feelings for so long, I realized that feeling in the moment was the only way I wanted to live.

I wouldn't have arrived at this point without further education. Anthropology and Gender Studies classes in college helped me understand how society affects individuals. I recognized how my unhappiness was related to specific gender roles and I then chose to express myself in new ways. There are other options, however, for achieving the same result. Emotional support from a young age and gender awareness in primary education can give people the confidence to discover how their own identity adheres or differs from sociocultural expectations. Children, teens, and young adults should understand that there are many positive ways to express oneself.

It is still very easy for me to fall into the old habit of repressing my feelings because I didn't learn how to express my own desires at a young age. Passivity was engrained into many of my responses, but I do my best to counteract this pattern by respectfully expressing my current feelings to others. I no longer question the legitimacy of my emotions because I realize that I cannot control them. I can accept my desires for what

they are—a part of living—and process them in healthy ways as they flow through me.

Processing these emotions means expressing them in my relationships. As a social being, I let people know how I am feeling. I allow them to better understand what I want, and I hope that they do the same with me. Even with negative emotions, I acknowledge why I am upset and it helps me find solutions. Most importantly, feeling in all moments reminds me that I am a living and growing individual.

• Do you feel capable of expressing how you feel on the inside?
• Do you feel that all emotional expression has to be demonstrated alone in private? If so, why do you feel that way?
• Do the people close to you try to restrict your expression of how you feel?
• What are some healthy ways of manifesting and expressing these feelings?
• Do your friends laugh at your jokes? Do they support you when you had a bad experience?

CARRY THIS YOU FOR A

MARK THE AMOUNT OF

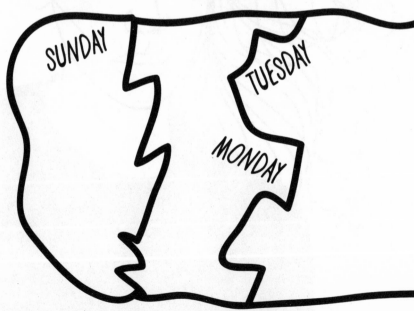

SUNDAY

TUESDAY

MONDAY

BOOK WITH FEW DAYS
TIMES YOU SAY SORRY

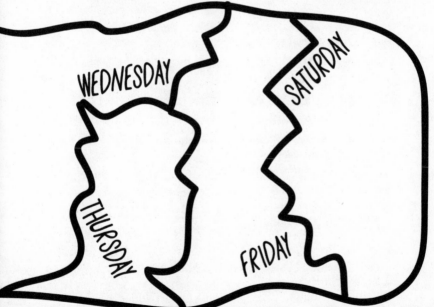

P-TALK FROM AN ADVENTURER

Independability by LZ

My past year was spent being intensely infatuated with someone who I thought was my friend, but as soon as things became slightly romantic, it dissolved as abruptly as sugar in water. They stopped talking to me completely after we had sex a couple of times. I didn't feel respected as a human being with thoughts, feelings, and opinions, and this broke my heart a bit. Clearly we weren't right for each other, but it took me a while to stop fantasizing about the potential of "us." I didn't want to be this person's girlfriend, but I thought we were building a meaningful relationship, a friendship. After this experience, some major introspection, objectiveness, and turning to my friends for guidance, I learned some lessons. My feelings were genuine and sweet for this person, and I'll never regret the experience. I know that I can care about someone deeply, and that's no small victory.

I don't know why this person cut off contact with me. Perhaps the situation had proved to be triggering or upsetting to them for some reason. I tried to explain that I only wanted to be friends. Perhaps they wanted to be lovers instead and couldn't deal with my vision. I won't know unless they get back in touch.

I'm an independent person. I love being alone. I've been alone most of my life, and I like it that way. I like going on adventures alone. I like having hobbies that don't require anyone else. That said, I still have meaningful relationships with other people. However, the most important relationship—and the one that is often neglected—is the one with yourself.

I'll admit, I still fall into the trap of societal expectation to be in a "romantic" relationship. It's malarkey, though. Being dependent on someone else is unhealthy and emotionally draining. It's okay to ask for help when you need it, but learn to be on your own, dammit. Do what you want to do for once.

1. Independability is the ability to be independent, autonomous, and rely on oneself. It's good to be alone.

Just because you're alone, it doesn't mean that you are lonely. Learning to rely on yourself and to use your own resources is empowering. You don't have to rely on other people or expect things from other people. It's healthy to self-soothe. Be free to think, feel, say, hear, and do what you want without the judgments or reactions of others. When you're with someone else, you might not go out and meet other people—being alone can help you meet people! Being single/alone also means you're strong enough to wait for what you deserve, in a "romantic" relationship, if you want one.

2. You don't need someone to fulfill you and/or fix you.

That unrealistic expectation is taught by films, family members, or society. There is no magical person who will fill all of those empty gaps inside you and make you whole or patch you up. No person is just going to swoop down and fix you. Imagine that kind of pressure! You need to be happy with and fix yourself.

We all need growth. Rely on yourself to face and solve your own problems. That will make you feel more attractive as a person.

3. Be present.

It's easy to be nostalgic. It's easy to get distracted by your phone, internet, social media, television, or whatever you find yourself doing. Getting caught up in other people's online lives is a time-suck that can be detrimental to your well-being. Think about where you are right now. Think about the good things about your life. Don't overwhelm yourself with things that you need to do later. Deal with things in front of you. Appreciate what's in front of you.

4. Stay busy.

If you're dealing with something painful, it's easy to get lazy and apathetic. Sometimes you need time to relax, but that alone won't make you feel better. Do something. Be productive. Figure out your goals. Allow yourself to reflect on your pain, but also be active so you don't just fester in the wound. Make a list of goals to accomplish in a year, in five years, in ten years. Don't stop dreaming. Apply yourself and stay determined. Go on adventures. Write the novel you've been meaning to. Take the trip that you've always wanted to go on! Paint that awesome portrait of your pet(s). Apply for that internship. Knit a sweater for your grandma. Don't lie in bed all day. Do something.

5. Remember who you are.

Remember this wonderful, unique, beautiful person in the mirror? Remember the hobbies you used to have? Take up the ones you want to again. Do what makes you happy. Don't let anyone dull your shine. Find the pleasures, dreams, goals, secrets, and habits that make you special. If you have great taste in literature, films, music, interior design, jewelry design—if you love playing an instrument, wood-crafting, bird watching, painting, skateboarding, surfing, snowboarding, being a dominatrix, etc.; if you're an animal lover, a human lover, an object lover, whatever makes you *you*—celebrate it! If you have a family or something similar, spend time with them. Family and good friends have a way of reminding you who you are.

6. Read.

Read a novel. Read a book of poetry. Read a zine. Read an article. Discover something new. Don't make an excuse. There are books for everyone out there. You learn so many lessons from reading. Experience is the best way, but learning from books is a good way to discover what you're excited about. Books are loyal friends who don't judge you, forget to call you back, or sleep with you and then stop talking to you.

7. Do something new.

Few things are more rewarding than challenging yourself to do a new activity. You'll gain self-confidence and realize you're stronger than you give yourself credit for. Enter a writing or art contest. Volunteer. It's great to help other people, and you'll find new purpose. You'll meet people who could have a positive influence on your life. Eat alone at a restaurant. Take a writing or woodshop class. Take a spin class, or a yoga class. See someone speak at a conference. You could get inspired. Hell, you can inspire yourself.

8. Let yourself grieve.

If you're reading this, it's likely that you're dealing with some shit right now. You're not alone. It's okay to break down, because those can lead to breakthroughs. Being vulnerable is not a sign of weakness. It takes strength to be honest and open with yourself or others. If you don't let the sad out, you'll bottle it up and repress it until it explodes, pouring out of you uncontrollably. Cry if you need or want to. Lay on your bed and cry. Go in your bathroom and cry. Go in your closet and cry. Go in a tree house and cry. Sit in your car and cry. Go wherever you feel safe, and be vulnerable. Write your thoughts or feelings in a journal. Paint on a canvas vigorously if you feel like it. Go to a park, lie in the grass, watch the clouds drift by, and contemplate life. Cry if you need to.

9. Do what you want.

I am giving you free license to do what you want (assuming you don't hurt anyone). You've earned it. Look, we all have responsibilities. We all have to do things we don't want to do but have to. Let go for a bit. Entertain yourself. Stop trying to please other people all of the time. Stop trying to get other people's approval, even important people in your life. Regret can be your friend or your nemesis. Let it be your friend who taught you the hard way, through experience. People regret more of the things they *didn't* do than the things they did. Get crazy and have fun, safely.

10. Indulge.

Find what gives you pleasure and allow yourself to enjoy it. Whether it's chocolate, masturbation, trashy films, binge watching Netflix, whatever. Wear your favorite clothes or accessories. Don't deny yourself something you really want (as long as you don't hurt anyone). Everything in moderation.

11. Dance it out.

When times are tough, sometimes you gotta dance it out. Put on music that makes you groove and dance in your underwear. If you haven't done this before, it makes *everything* a whole lot better. Look in the mirror. See how beautiful and fun you are. You can be as silly or sexual or daring as you want to be. Embrace it.

CONSENSUALITY

12. Be Your Own Best Friend.

You can't always rely on someone to catch you when you fall, so learn to catch yourself. Be kind to yourself. Self-loathing is an obstacle that prevents you from doing anything. At the end of the day, you are the only person who has to live with yourself. So love yourself. Forgive yourself. Get in touch with your feelings. Talk to yourself; it's okay!

Final Note

If you're going through something painful, know that it happens to everybody sometimes. If a relationship recently ceased to exist, it's not the end of the world. It just feels like it right now.

You're going to be okay.
You will be happy again.
Hell, you're going be better than ever.

PRAISE LOG

{ Use this space to write down any compliments you receive.
Come back to this page when you feel uninspired. }

LIST WHAT YOU LOVE

MAKE GOALS

RESENTFUL

After realizing that much of my regret was due to my socialization within emotional gender roles, I felt frustrated. I was deeply disturbed by the **privilege** that many men held in personal relationships. I had to understand who I was outside all of the regret, but I initially couldn't see past the anger. Resentment towards men and "masculine" personalities had grown within me for years. Resentment expanded even more in my relationships when issues went unresolved and power inequalities remained intact. Saying "sorry" millions of times had watered an immense garden of anger and frustration.

My thoughts sometimes trailed slightly behind my realization that I had control over my own life. They would stop and throw tantrums like little children, instead of expressing their true maturity. They were the anxiety and resentment that I was taught to have in matters of men. But they did not come from feminism. They stemmed from being taught that men would judge me for my body, that men would not like me if I was too assertive about my sexuality, and that men would disrespect me if I "gave it up" too quickly. They came from being taught that I would need a dominant man to take care of me, a man to be "the man," a man who would outwardly control me.

These feelings came from living in a patriarchal society where men, good or bad, were more powerful than women. I learned from many outlets—family, news, movies—that women should be protected by men, and that if the "good men" weren't around, I could be attacked by the "bad ones." Women should not feel that they need to carry pepper spray or yield their keys as weapons when they are out and alone at night, but stories of rape and assault leave every woman on guard. Any time that I had to walk home in the dark by myself, I would run due to my fear. Any time I had plans to travel alone, I would invite someone out of what I thought was necessity. Any time a boy showed interest, I assumed that I had to play hard to get if I wanted him to respect me. I, like many females, had been trained to blindly believe in the power men could have over me.

The inhibitions that I learned in childhood continued to challenge my personal wants and needs. They shouted worries of becoming too involved with men. They told me that all of my feelings were wrong, that only desperate women put themselves in danger by expressing their sexual desire. I was taught to distrust half of humanity, and as a result, I learned

to distrust my feelings for that humanity. Instead of trusting myself, I played into the roles that patriarchy had cast for me. Male authority figures, even my own male partners, felt like a threat to me. The large amount of power they had within our patriarchal society made it easy to blame individual men for societal problems.

Despite having the physical and emotional ability to disagree with the people who encouraged sexist gender roles, I generally avoided the debate. Despite knowing well-intentioned males with sides that aren't brutish and disrespectful, my anxiety and resentment held me back from communicating with them. Despite being an intelligent woman who knows what I want in this world, I always felt insecure when my gender preferences were questioned.

Whether it was whom I wanted to be with or how I wanted to be with them, people showed concern for my desires that fell outside of their idea of a straight female. One close family member cried over my interest in a woman. Others told me that the reason I had relationship problems was because I wasn't dating manly enough men. It went beyond unsupportive. Each disapproval was a reminder of the judgment I'd receive if I didn't follow the rules of heterosexual dating. These imprinted emotions of mainstream beliefs threatened to disable me in matters of love, and tried to push me back onto a prescribed path.

But these false emotions only distracted me from what I know is the truth: there is good in humanity when we learn to respect each other. When I move closer to my personal goals and meet people who share my value for equality, the doubts from my past appear less and less. Though many men may not consider inequality a problem because they do not see how it affects them, many other men are aware of gender issues and would like to help combat inequality. When I write and publicly display my confidence, the insecurities lose their control. I see how I do not need to be accepted by men in order to accept myself. Now, when I tell someone that I love them, the honesty frees me. After learning that everything I previously hated about myself wasn't legitimate, those children throwing tantrums are finally growing up.

My parents taught me that you shouldn't talk about your exes, but a large part of growing up was discovering what worked best for me. I always maintained some sort of communication with or about my previous partners after the break-up, and it was examining the problems in past relationships that eventually allowed me to trust men. If discussion about a past relationship helps to rebuild health, continued communication is never a failure. And even when a relationship is destructive, it never helps to have family or friends shaming someone for their interactions with a person.

I don't know anyone who completely stops communicating with and about their ex immediately after a break up. There are so many lingering feelings at the end of a relationship. You and your previous

partner(s) are going to have frustration with each other, whether you express it or not. It helps to talk about these feelings. It's painful to revisit these memories, but in the end, I never regret it. It took years of being mad at myself and resentful towards previous partners to learn that there wasn't a definite end in relationships.

Sometimes it is necessary and healthy to completely stop talking to someone. Personal safety and health is always a priority. If a previous partner or friend feels that it is in their best interest to stop talking to you, *you need to respect that.* This doesn't mean, however, that all communication about the previous relationship needs to stop. In these cases, you can still learn from your past by communicating with a counselor, friends, or your family. Examine what you've learned from your previous relationships.

Love—Another Word for Insanity?

While revisiting feelings from my past relationships, I discovered a journal entry that I wrote when I was 18 years old:

Men are evil. They make women go crazy. But then again, they probably think the same thing about women. It is a shame that love can't be simple. Maybe it is and I haven't experienced it yet. I doubt it though.
Love is just another word for insanity.

The highs and lows of romantic relationships can feel like insanity. The dysfunctional couple is so common that we can all immediately understand what that looks like and means. I've lived it and it's all too likely that you have too.

Friends and family have witnessed me closing myself off in relationships. There was one instance where the person I was with would argue with me and I would hide in emotional turmoil (silent treatment), hating him and myself for our deteriorating feelings. Our loved ones tried to help and hoped it was better behind closed doors. Truth be told, it was great at times, but there was nothing to keep us from pinballing back and forth in frustration. I was convinced that our "craziness" was a side effect of being young.

Starting a relationship can be incredibly fun; I have always loved the beginnings of my relationships. But each time it quickly became my priority to keep the "honeymoon phase" intact. I thought apologizing incessantly would help; however, all it did was hold the conflict inside, waiting to come out on another day. After the conflict had been kept inside for too long, forming sentences to describe how I felt became a feat. When I was depressed, I couldn't process my emotions internally, let alone explain them to someone else. It felt like it was too late. It felt like no one could understand me, so I resorted to silence.

When I would get stuck in believing no one understood me, it was easy to see gender stereotypes. Guys were jerks. Girls were bitchy. The "us against them" mentality infiltrated my depression, and "them" could be men or women at polarized ends of the gender spectrum. It became difficult to love without

resentment in sexual and platonic relationships. In my mind, everyone became the girly girl or the manly man. I couldn't see past my judgments to develop relationships with others. When I had extreme negative emotions, I cut ties and pushed people away. I saw no way to repair the resentment, anger, and sadness. I would try to replace the relationships, but I did not know how to repair my view of other people.

Among my classmates in college, I saw how there was a negative connotation associated with women's studies, so I avoided courses on gender. I didn't want to be the girl in class who always pointed out, "What about the women?" I thought I could ignore power dynamics in relation to gender and emotions. But I needed to explore alternative environments, where people had different views of gender, to begin forming healthy relationships. I needed to understand that there is always an alternative way to do something.

Thankfully, I had to take a course on gender to fulfill a requirement for my major, anthropology. After the course, I began to understand the possibilities of gender. I learned how people could express gender in different ways and I began to understand the possibilities in my own relationships. I realized how necessary it was to find a new understanding of relationships, so that my love could be healthy, supportive, and balanced.

Courses on gender deepened my understanding of privilege within relationships. I used to think that social norms always caused more suffering for women than men; however, it became clear over time that gender norms hurt all people by limiting acceptable forms of expression. Whether we have white privilege, male privilege, straight privilege, or any other trait that society arbitrarily elevates, we can examine how our privilege hurts others and live our lives in a way that attempts to reduce suffering.

More and more, I have thought about how society treats people who do not fit into traditional gender roles. People of every gender are forced to struggle with societal expectation. In small and large ways, strict ideas of masculinity can jeopardize equality among all of us.

Examples of Unexpected Inequality in the Battle of the Sexes

1. Dating

One of the men I dated for a short period of time brought to my attention the double bind of being a progressive male. Though he was liberal and theoretically supportive of feminism, he constantly tried to become the provider in our relationship. He believed that the failure of his last relationship was due to his inability to financially support his ex-girlfriend. He felt disappointed with himself anytime that I paid for a meal. Though I told him that I was happy to pay for our dates, his self-esteem suffered because he could never fulfill his masculine expectations. He felt that he had to reach a certain level of financial security to be a successful human. By doing so, he abandoned his individual talents as a writer and artist to pursue the more "manly" venture of computer science. We did not continue our relationship for long, so I cannot testify to his happiness now. But I can recognize how our society disproportionately rewards male-dominated career choices to the detriment of those who choose an alternative path.

2. Sexual Orientation

Another friend suffered in his relationships due to societal views of sexuality. Raised in a household with Judeo-Christian views of gender and **sexual orientation**, he suppressed his feelings for other men. Though his female partner accepted his attraction to men, he continually struggled and failed to understand his own sexuality. It was difficult for him to reconcile his identity as a man with his bisexuality. He knew others who challenged current notions of male sexuality; however, his upbringing barred him from accepting his own sexual desires. For those raised in an environment that restricts sexuality, it's difficult to understand the diversity of sexuality in the world.

3. Gender Expression

In one of my gender studies courses, a **transgender** man detailed how he had seen the world from both sides of the traditional gender binary. He experienced being called stupid and dependent by his ex-husband when he was female-bodied. Despite liking kids and having grandchildren himself, he experienced mothers steering their children away from him because he was a middle-aged man. He saw how his life was restricted on both sides of the gender divide, but also recognized that he generally experienced more privilege as a man in social interactions.

It took years for him to realize that if he wasn't being himself, he would be severely depressed. Before he started talking about his struggles and living as himself, he had multiple suicide attempts and was on multiple medications for various mental health issues. It was hard enough making changes in how I thought about my emotional responses within my female identity, so I can only imagine how painful it was for him to have virtually everything about his gender identity feel wrong. The perspective of someone perceived as more than one gender should truly be valued, just as everyone's perspective is to be valued.

The men described above suffered to varying degrees, partially because they denied their non-traditional traits. At some point in their lives, they realized that it was considered degrading for a man to act like a woman. To combat negative beliefs towards women, it's necessary for men to express how patriarchy affects their lives. The journey from regret to respect is a long one. We're socialized to be concerned about how others see us, rather than to take the initiative and learn about how individuals prefer to present themselves. If we're socialized in different ways early on, we learn to respect others and ourselves instead of regretting who we are.

How do you react when you feel resentful towards a current/previous partner?

Have you allowed traditional gender roles to affect your judgment of another person? If so, write about these experiences.

What have you learned from exploring your past relationships/experiences?

A LEARNING EXPERIENCE FROM A CO-ADVENTURER

Maroon Menemy & Me By Robert

My experiences with romance and sex are limited, yet I do possess a human heart that has travailed an extensive gamut of emotions that grants me a contributing voice to this book. When I began to liberate myself from the psychologically enforced asexuality in which I was "living," I relished in the dissolution of an imposed contract I had made with my old cretin nemesis, otherwise known as traditional masculinity. For a while, I blamed traditional masculinity for my eventual friend-break-up with a guy I had the worst-ever crush on. I thought that from the moment that I had told him that I "was in love with him" his testes warned him that I was a threat to his masculinity, and should be avoided. It seemed easy to ignore my faulty interpersonal skills and blame an abstract, social construction for my unrequited erotic desires; however, I eventually realized that the problem between us had existed since I had first met him the year previous, when I would still torture myself with inauthentic asexuality.

Getting dressed in the locker room after swim practice, I was obsessing over the usual stressors, lost in the sea of worries about school. Then I noticed him, just sitting on the bench, looking beautiful and pensive, as if changing from his maroon speedo into everyday clothes had made him discover a hidden truth about humanity and its place in the universe.

As I was drying myself, he plainly struck up a conversation with me, and asked me if I wanted to hang out with him. As I would do in those days, (a habit which I'm sure led to my eventual mental breakdown) I quickly suppressed the floods of desire, ecstasy, and hunger that crammed for a push at my loins. I could not believe this guy wanted to socialize with a nondescript person such as myself. In the dead voice that my vocal chords used to produce, I introduced myself and said that yes, I would most certainly want to hang out with him. And we did.

We would talk about nothing but swim and school. That year, I was at the top of my game, passionate about everything in life, or at least the parts I wasn't trying to suffocate. Our friendship was at its best when we were both driven and motivated. It pains me to remember those days. Suffice it to say, what I felt when I would sit in his car and talk to him was the bliss of a food coma, when one is lying in bed and suddenly wants to hug someone with brown eyes and a bright blue jacket.

And then the end began. Finals week of 2012, I became extremely stressed out about exams, my uncle's illness, and my nasty spat with my mom. He appeared out of the blue and asked me what was going on. I told him about my preoccupations, and my eyes began to well up. He comforted me, and said, "Come here" as we hugged for the first time.

I would like to pause and excavate the thoughts that came up in those five seconds. Masculine models of affection between men are difficult to please when it comes to hugging. These days, I fantasize about men greeting me with a kiss on my hand, keeping their lips pressed to my skin dutifully until a slight nod or smile assents their separation. Back then, however, I merely wondered what it would mean for him to hug me if he knew that I had a crush on him. Weirdly, I thought that my fabrications of sexual quasi-nonexistence were working, as he was unabashedly offering, even if in this slight manner, his body for my comfort. I figured, in my unenlightened mind, that he wouldn't do so if he suspected that I was (am) hot for a male-male arrangement. Beneath all of the desire, disruption, and chaos that this hug shook up in me, I was grateful that this guy had flipped the middle finger to traditional masculinity even if for a moment.

But yes, the beginning of the end it was. Summer came and went, and brought along autumn. We were temporarily distanced, a time during which my sexuality decided that ten years of being stifled was quite enough, thank you. We suddenly hung out again when my brain was about to implode and I was in dire necessity to speak with someone. He was the first human being besides my first therapist to whom I expressed my desires for males. I did it indirectly, only saying that I had a "secret" I needed to let out; else I'd become insane. He put two and two together right away. We had a deep talk in his car, after which he offered me another one of his signature hugs. I suppose I am privileged to have had such a beautiful human being to partake in such a monumental part of my personal history.

But the increasing intimacy I was sharing with him caused too much of a strain on what I assumed was his framework of masculinity. My eventual emotional crises (the worst of which he witnessed) and mental frailty caused me to adopt the traditionally feminized binary to him. I acted dependent and presume he found that to be a complement. I felt like maintaining our friendship would become too allegorical to a romantic relationship. As 2013 progressed, the winter crawled into a grave, and so did our friendship. I harbored feelings of hatred, disgust, envy, passion, desire, love-lust, and a little more desire for him, while he slowly began to be apathetic towards me, and wary of beginning conversation, lest I tell him of my struggles. I sent him one e-mail in the summer that he never responded to, and I have not seen him ever since, and probably will never again.

For a long time, I blamed our discrepant relationships to masculinity for the demise of our friendship. I bitterly thought that all of my heterosexual male friends would leave me as he did. Eventually, painfully realized that my overdependence on his emotional support was the reason he decided I was unfit to remain in his life. At the end of the day, we were just two human beings all along; the fact that we are both males was only relevant to me, who desired him sexually. I am almost certain he did not care at all whether our relationship was "too allegorical of a

 54

romantic one." My own fixations and anxieties pushed him away. If anything, he tired of me as a person, not me as a threat to heteronormativity. He was my friend through my worst moments when I was convinced that suicide was the only solution to avoid disappointing my parents and losing my mother's love. He just happened to ease naturally into his masculinity; i.e., he wasn't a "product of society" as I would try to dismiss him. I let go of my resentment towards "typically" masculine men, for he never associated with me in obedience to traditional masculinity. He had genuinely desired my company.

In order to best combat gender expression restraints, we should pretend they don't exist, and do away with militant, angry efforts against them. If we pretend that traditional gender expression expectations don't exist, we will be happy and accepting of ourselves, and not wrongly assume things about other people, or their motivations for being nice to us. Believe me, as one who has been offended repeatedly for not acting "masculine," it took me a long time to approach this problem with a peace-filled agenda in mind. We should disarticulate the criteria that outlines what behaviors connote masculinity or femininity; if we resist these conveniences even slightly, there is so much more that we can learn about someone's personality.

Just as there are billions of people on earth, there are billions of **gender expressions**, the intricacies of which cannot be denied. My ex-friend's masculinity was a beautiful and complex union between his body and his world. It was by no means "patriarchal," nor did it snuggle against the walls of the "traditional masculinity" wooden chest. His delicate frame housed one of the strongest and most determined personalities I have ever known.

I remember us hanging out at a fragrance store in the mall and as I was looking for a gift for my mom, I thought that the cult of beauty-as-a-female-prerogative would bar him from enjoying this store with me. I was mistaken; he was cutely skipping around, smelling and rubbing lotions on his slender hands. Then he chirped, "This one smells like marshmallow!" Never since have I encountered such sweet manhood in an individual; no one's lungs have been capable of inhaling "femininity" and exhaling—not homophobic remarks or anxieties—but simple joviality.

A year later, he bought a cherry lotion because it was three dollars (I used to duly call him my pragmatist.) Such an economical choice sparked quite a humorous, homo-social exchange in the locker room a few days later. As everyone was changing and what have you, his fragrance suddenly just decided to stimulate and seduce my olfactory pores (talk about consent!). In any event, I was apparently not the only one thus disrupted, for someone exclaimed, "Damn! I smells like fine ass bitches in here!" at which point my ex-friend and I exchanged a knowing grin, for only knew that it was in fact his cherry-exuding epidermis that was provoking lustful desires in this manly space.

A similar occurrence took place when accompanied him to choose a Christmas tree for his family. The customer service guy asked us in all seriousness if it was our first tree. We laughed and said no, but I couldn't stop thinking the whole day what it would be like if it were true. I know that some people condemn fairy-tale notions of relationships, but sometimes it is these whose cheap ambrosia feed our most hedonistic, painfully exquisite fantasies when we are alone at night and would rather not cry ourselves to sleep. I invoked all the corniness possible, and imagined us decorating the tree as our hands would meet periodically.

Alas, life shot a huge harpoon at all of the psychological mess I made of this non-relationship, and woke up the next day knowing how impossible such a situation would be. Furthermore, I realized that there would have been even more illusions to be murdered f I looked for men with whom it would be possible to have a relationship. I thought to myself, "Life is tough and I would rather not find out how much more tough t can be by having an actual domestic relationship with someone. I would rather suffer alone than learn the truth."

I used to obsess over the structures of masculinity and its power over men. I used to ask 'Why did he talk to me in the locker room? Why does he want to hang out with me? Does he no suspect that my enforced asexuality is becoming too exhaustive to sustain the longer I am around him; the more I have voyeuristic displays of his dripping wet body?" After months of solitude, severe depression, and reflection, I concluded that sometimes people are not as our intellectual egos may wish them to be, and authentically appreciate the person inside of us. He was the first "ally" I ever had, even without my knowing that he had surmised my then-secret. I embrace and love heterosexual people who are conscious of the struggles of their fellow human beings; nonetheless, I wish to become my own ally, and embody a sort of simplicity of heart towards other people for the sake of peace, one that respects the intellectual limitations of others and myself.

RESPECTFUL

After examining gender and race critically in school, I began to understand how differences in societal power shape our relationships. We live with an idea of what is normal. It can make us feel forced to live in environments that degrade people who are labeled as different. Thankfully, there are also ways to create safe spaces, which I now like to think of as environments of *consensuality.*

Our family history, our gender, our privilege or lack of privilege, our emotions, our boundaries, they all contribute to how we understand consent. These issues influence how comfortable we feel in different intimate interactions, so it's important to consider all of these topics when learning about consent. In my first three years of sexual activity, I did not know how consent functioned in sexual situations. I was aware that consenting meant saying "yes," but I never invoked consent as an assertion of my agency during sex. I would either say "no" or engage in the sexual activity.

Two years later and in a serious relationship, I began to realize how it had become harder to say "no" to my partner. The mood of the sex seemed to switch. I became some sort of resentful gatekeeper for the sex that he wanted. Many of the interactions are foggy in my recollections, but I remember the feelings. Sometimes, we would be drunk or angry. In addition, sex became physically painful at times. I noticed that my bodily reactions often corresponded with my comfort level.

One instance, however, remains clear in my memory. I will always remember the time that he continued having sex with me after I said no. He was behind me and I was on all fours (i.e. doggy style). I honestly hated this position. One of my current boundaries is that my partner and I cannot have sex in this position. But it was the only way that my past boyfriend would orgasm. In this instance, it became painful and I asked him to stop. He continued having sex with me. Even after expressing that I was in pain, I had to physically push him off of me to end the interaction.

I think this moment is imprinted in my mind because it was closest to my previous understanding of rape. The moment clearly resembled assault to me because he continued having sex with me after I said no. At this time, my only reference for **sexual assault** was the crimes I had seen reported by local news. Rape meant a stranger attacking a young woman and having sex with her, despite her struggle and resistance. I still wasn't able to recognize the sexual assault within my own relationship, but I felt its effects. I was extremely preoccupied with rape in a destructive way. I felt that somehow at some point in my life, I was going to be raped if I wasn't careful.

I assumed that my fear was irrational and my responsibility alone. Because external influences often painted this male-female power dynamic as "normal" in sexual relationships, I felt like something was wrong with me. I broke up with my boyfriend eventually, but even then, I did not directly relate our interactions to sexual assault. I left the relationship simply because I felt trapped and insecure while with him. I continued to feel vulnerable to sexual assault after the break-up and decided to sign up for a self-defense class in hopes that it would help me feel more secure.

In the first portion of this class, we talked about consent as the act of saying "yes!" to sex. This insight initially made me worry that something was wrong with me. I had sometimes felt violated even if I had agreed to a sexual interaction. My boundaries had still been crossed somehow. These situations usually involved a "yes" borne out of social obligation or pressure. My boyfriend had often asked to have sex over and over again until my initial "no" turned into a "yes." I recognized that there had moments where I had sex with my boyfriend when I didn't want to, meaning that we had had non-consensual sex. I also knew that many of my friends had similar experiences with their boyfriends. It appeared that some men felt

they had a right to a certain amount of sex purely because they were in a relationship.

The verbal portion of the self-defense course helped me connect the dots and realize that my fear of rape was related to a sexual obligation that my boyfriend had imposed on me. I recognized that my boyfriend had exerted control over my body. I grasped a new understanding of sexual assault and how it could occur within relationships. While previously I imagined rape and sexual assault as unwanted sex that occurred outside of a relationship, **sexual assault** actually occurs anytime a person does not willingly consent to a sexual act.

It's important to look at consent as a process within relationships. For this reason, the term "sexual assault" more accurately represents actual experiences and the range of effects that follow. Because "rape" is a loaded word with a huge history that usually implies women or "weak men" as the victims, people may be hesitant to describe their experiences as rape. Sexual assault can be used to describe a variety of violations and does not necessarily apply to a specific gender.

My boyfriend and I got back together once more. I was much more vocal about how previous **sexual abuse** within our relationship had affected me. He was very understanding for a time being, but our patterns were hard to break. Our sex drives were incompatible and neither of us felt completely comfortable in the relationship. While we only participated in consensual sex during our second attempt at a loving relationship, he often became angry or annoyed by my effort to exert more control over my body.

He wanted to go back to how things were before, but I knew how unhealthy it was to participate in non-consensual sex. Consent was no longer about saying yes or no. It was and still is about creating an environment where it is ok to say yes or no. When I felt violated, it was because I wasn't in an environment where I felt safe expressing my wants. Whether it was someone disregarding my initial no, intimidating me into believing that it was an obligation, or manipulating me emotionally in some other way, the issue was that I wasn't in a safe and comfortable environment. In any intimate interaction, all parties should feel like they can communicate their desires. Consent is about respecting each other and creating environments where people feel comfortable stating their desire.

Examples of Disrespect

1. A Stranger

On a study-abroad trip to Spain, I decided that I would push my personal boundaries. Though I didn't even feel comfortable going to a restaurant alone in my own hometown, I wanted to try exploring the city of Salamanca by myself. I went into debt for the trip, so I might as well experience the city to its fullest.

I began a walk across the city. Nothing too daunting, just searching for some city-views and good conversation with locals. After stopping for a bit in a busy park, an older man approached me and

began speaking in Spanish. I don't remember what he asked exactly, but I remember feeling like he was my grandfather. He seemed interested to know about my studies and I was excited to practice Spanish with a local.

We began walking towards the center of the city, La Plaza Mayor. I felt fairly secure with the large amount of people all around us, until he began asking things I didn't understand and tried to steer me towards a less populated corner of a street. In an attempt to be polite, I tried to say goodbye and thank you for the conversation. He became more forceful with his intentions, pressing his body against me. While I was unable to move and in complete shock, he kissed me and groped my breast. I desperately pushed my way back towards the crowd and ultimately ended the encounter by running from him.

On my way back to my room, I cried. Later, I tried to convince myself it was a misunderstanding. Now, I realize that misunderstanding or not, the man molested me without regard for my feelings and boundaries. Unfortunately, the occurrence crushed my self-esteem into a juvenile understanding of strangers, but understanding consent allowed me to ensure that I personally never caused the same level of discomfort for another person.

Someone, we'll call him Jeremy, asked for my number and email. We had a nice conversation at a bar and appeared to have similar interests—he said he wanted to work on my feminist zine with me—but it was not clear whether we would be more than friends. I sent him an email for clarification.

Me: Hey, I just started dating someone and I felt like I should let you know before we hang out. Sorry I didn't tell you sooner! I wasn't sure where it was going with the other person, and I still don't have it all figured out, but I felt like I should let you know. If you want to hang out, I think it would be a lot of fun! Let me know if we're on for tomorrow.

Jeremy: Oh ok, I wasn't trying to fuck you anyway; I would've but I don't want to be your bf so whatevers. I'll try not to let you cheat but I'm irresistible when wasted.

Me: Believe me; I wish I didn't have to give a disclaimer every time I met someone of the opposite sex just because I'm dating someone, but I don't want to be misleading. Whether your email was a joke or not, I think you should reconsider how you think about drunk sex. A person can't give consent if

he/she is incoherent. As long as you both agree to it, I hope you can have a nice fuck/friendship/relationship with the next girl you meet.

Jeremy : Regardless, I'm still down to hang out tomorrow. I'll call you.

I declined. His response to the news that I was dating someone else had shown me that he did not care about my decisions. I felt like he needed to know that he had crossed important boundaries. His view of sex blatantly disrespected my right to consent.

3. A Friend/Previous Sexual Partner

I was often invited to get drinks and sushi with my friend, we'll call him Trevor. Without asking what I wanted or even if I wanted anything, he usually ordered our first round of drink specials, which meant a small sake and a Sapporo for each of us. I wanted that first round, though after round one, it became harder to say yes or no.

One of these times out, it dawned on me that something was wrong. I had actually met with him to show him an essay I had written on gender inequalities, yet he completely ignored my ability to order my own drinks. It irked me that he took it upon himself to make the decision for me. When another round of drinks was ordered without my consent, I told him that I didn't want any more. I said no, but the next round of drinks came anyway. I was completely ignored. The server never questioned his request. I felt incredibly uncomfortable refusing the drinks.

At the end of the night, I said no when he invited me back to his house. I ignored his last attempts to change my mind as I got on the bus to my house. I realized from prior experiences with Trevor that there was a possibility of him coercing me into sex if I crashed at his place. The times that I had stayed at his house in the past, the times that I didn't say no, I also wasn't able to say yes. Consent was not possible after I was intoxicated. He took the limbo of drunkenness as consent, but it was nowhere close to a consensual interaction. I wish that I hadn't had to be hyper-vigilant when going out for drinks. I also wish that I could have continued my friendship with Trevor without fear of sexual assault. Ultimately, I wasn't able to achieve a respectful relationship with him.

Alcohol holds an ambiguous role in our society. It can be a social activity, a destructive force, and a fun pastime all at once. It can impair our judgment and change our views temporarily. As far as Trevor goes, he was a close friend with an alcohol problem that destroyed many of his relationships.

These men aren't the only people who assume consent. We all must work to understand when a situation is non-consensual and recognize the personhood of those we hurt. Nothing, whether alcohol, privilege, or another corrupted tool of power, should be used to blur consent. Nothing should keep a person from making their own decisions about their body and life. Consent can only truly be given when someone is in a safe environment and sober state of mind. If a person's judgment is impaired or if you haven't respectfully asked what they want, you can't ensure their consensual participation in the activity. Assuming or ignoring consent is an abuse of power.

Sex Ed Revisited

We need to talk about "it." You know, "doing it," "making love," "fucking," and my least favorite, "getting lucky." Looking at these sexual euphemisms already gives us an idea of what we're up against. Our words can evoke romance, vulgarity, passivity. "Getting lucky" is my least favorite because it counteracts **agency** (one's ability to act). When sex is left to luck, no one is responsible for the interaction.

Verbal and visual ideas of sex will always exist in mainstream culture, but clear discussions about healthy relationships, sexuality, and gender are much harder to find. Even within progressive circles, these are issues that need to be reconsidered when we interact with each other. We need to take action and learn more about healthy sexual interactions. We are all responsible for creating an environment of consent, which means communicating with one another about the following issues:

- What is the difference between sexual orientation and gender?

- How are my relationships affected by power and privilege?

- Do you feel comfortable talking about sex?

- Do you feel comfortable having sex?

- What do I do if I unintentionally cross someone's boundaries in an emotional and/or sexual relationship?

- What kind of a relationship are you looking for, if any?

When discussing these issues as a community, begin broadly. Discover how your friends, family, or co-adventurers view gender and sexual orientation. Stretch the boundaries of each other's knowledge. Learn new terms like **cisgender**—a person whose gender expression matches the sex assigned to them at birth. Explore how the answers to these questions can change your understanding of sex and life. Don't try to logically separate the sexual components; you'll ignore the related issues of boundaries and gender. If you state how you feel honestly and are open to these discussions, you'll begin diving into the many layers of healthy relationships.

In specific situations, the first place to go to with questions about sex is the person/people involved in the interaction. The communal conversation, however, should have begun long before that. Community education on sex needs to allow for discussion. If students/community members can't ask questions, sex-ed becomes stagnant and limited to the current authority's view of sex.

I often find that gender is the missing component in general sex-ed. When we talk about female anatomy and male anatomy in high school classrooms, there is rarely a discussion about the different types of people connected to these sexual organs. The result is an assumption that a male-bodied person will act like a "man" and a female-bodied person will act like a "woman." Gender studies departments at universities and counter-culture publications often attempt to change the misconception of universal sex-gender correspondence (cisgender), but information on alternative genders is not distributed to most people.

One of my college professors encouraged us to create our own gender spectrum. She drew a line with the female symbol on the right side and the male symbol on the left side, and asked us to write actions on the board in the correct location of the spectrum. Our actions ranged from "brushing teeth," placed in the middle of the spectrum, to "painting nails" and "playing football" on opposite sides of the board. None of the actions had to do with a person's biological **sex**, rather they matched our cultural perceptions of the genders: women and men.

After we had written our actions on the board, she asked us to place ourselves on the spectrum. A clump of women marked their spots just to the right of the male-female boundary. One male and a few females placed themselves in the center of the spectrum. The other men lingered close to the border on the male side. A few females joined them, crossing the gender divide despite their biological sex. Only a small percentage of the class was scattered at the ends of the spectrum. Most of us clung to gender neutrality, preferring to disconnect our identities from being just a woman or just a man. My professor pointed out how it was less likely for men to recognize their feminine traits on the spectrum, but also recognized that each year more students of all genders migrated to the middle of the spectrum.

Even a gender spectrum that places "feminine" and "masculine" on opposite ends is becoming increasingly outdated, as the characteristics given to these categories are often based on traditional values. In other courses, I discovered how people could incorporate systems outside of our traditional gender binary into their community. In many cultures, there is a third gender. Research Tombois in West Sumatra and Fa'afafine in Samoa to discover just two of the many other genders existing in the world. You'll be amazed by the variety of gender expressions that go beyond a person's biological sex.

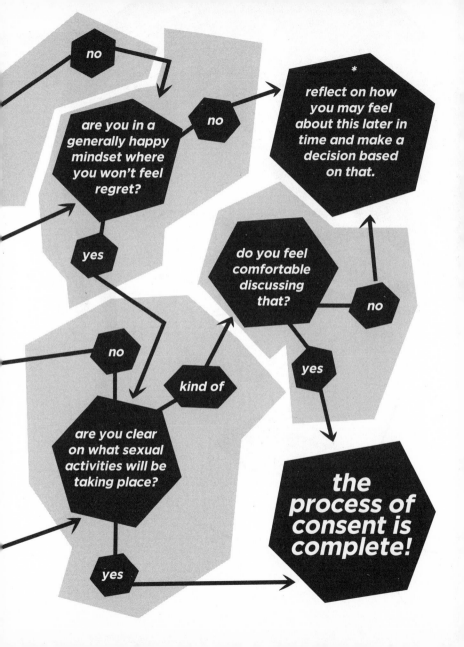

STEREOTYPICAL GENDER SPECTRUM

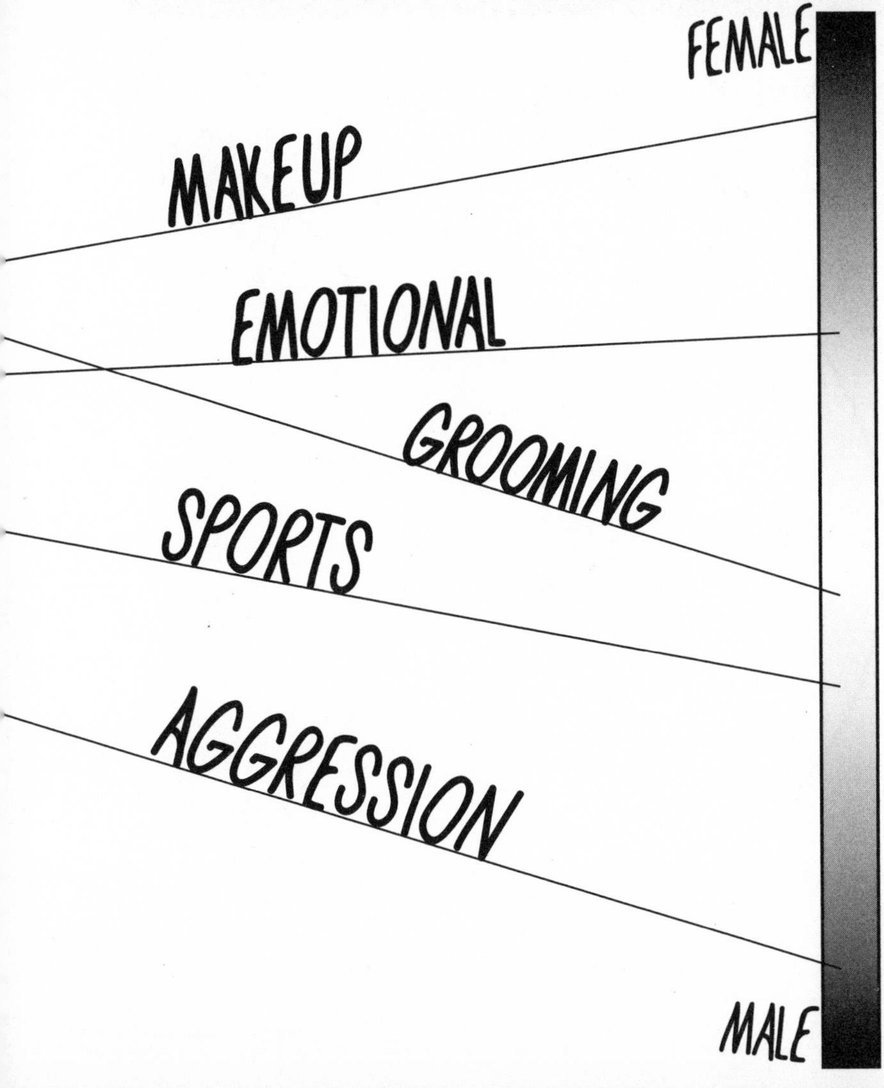

CREATE YOUR OWN GENDER SPECTRUM

where do YOU fall?

FEMININE

FEMALE

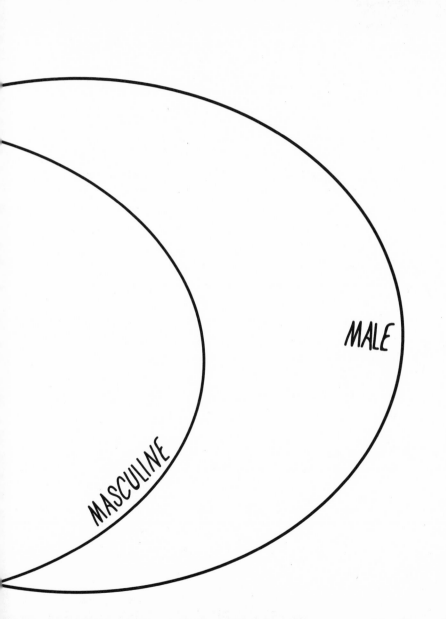

Additional culturally acceptable gender categories can sometimes create safer environments for those who do not categorize themselves as a man or a woman.

In addition, emotions or lack of emotions surrounding sex should be considered. We often tell women that they will become attached to their partner after sex and will desire exclusive relationships, while men are viewed as being prone to polygamy and able to have sex without emotional ties. The myth of an emotional gender divide perpetuates itself in conservative environments where there are less open discussions about sex; however, it is not the primary narrative in people's sexual experiences. There is no primary narrative for any category of person. The important part in allowing feelings to become a part of the discussion is that it shows how sexual experiences have different emotional effects per individual.

CONSIDER THIS

It is rude to assume someone's gender by their presentation and downright impossible to understand a person's view of sexuality and gender from their age, length of their skirt, haircut, or any other external representation. There is so much that goes into how we view sexuality and gender; the only real way to find out what these concepts mean is to talk about them.

Try bringing one of these topics up the next time you see your family. Who knows, your grandparents may surprise you.

AN INSIGHT FROM A CO-ADVENTURER

Learning How To Respect Myself and Others By Abner

As a result of disability, I became a daily bus commuter for the first time at age 36. It's been one of the most illuminating experiences in my life to watch how people behave around strangers, test boundaries, respect each other's time and privacy, and employ various methods of deflection.

You see everything imaginable, from people willing to go to tremendous lengths to avoid any kind of interaction with a stranger to people who are equally entitled and will shoulder their way into a stranger's conversation. One day, a boy in his twenties asked me what my disability was. Receiving weekly reminders about my right to privacy and constantly reflecting on my own boundaries, I found the question to be rude and so I told him that I'd rather not talk about it. To my surprise, he responded, "It's okay. I understand. Don't feel bad. I have a disability too. I have Asperger's Syndrome. Do you know what that is?"

I know all too well about Asperger's Syndrome (A.S.). I was diagnosed with it at age 30. It saddened me deeply that he referred to it as a disability but it did explain his lack of tact and respect for social mores. I can understand and respect why he'd bring it up to a stranger to sort of say, "I'm sorry. I just can't help that I'm like this. I really do try."

You say, "I'm sorry" a lot when you have Asperger's and it's painfully in keeping with my own experience.

Asperger's wasn't accepted into psychology until the 1990s, when I was too old to be screened for it and since I've never had biological children to inherit A.S., I hadn't been screened for it until I mentioned to the right therapist that I continually "missed" people's nonverbal expressions of their boundaries. But I had done much damage to the relationships around me already before I received my diagnosis at age 30 and had a road map to effective management.

Prior to my diagnosis, my therapist and I had been deadlocked for six months, without any real progress. She was always frustrated with me and would say things like "You really have to do your part if you want this to work." And by that, she meant that she didn't feel like I was coming in prepared or putting in enough effort to analyze the events of the previous week and my contributions that resulted in conflict. I really tried. I would remember every bit of conflict that happened between our twice weekly two hour appointments, but I had socially isolated myself and didn't always have that much conflict, so we instead spent months talking about every bit of hardship in my childhood, analyzing the ways that I'd been treated, how I was reserved with people now as a result, and things that were under my own control and agency, and how to handle them better. At first I was very much like a lost, wandering puppy, in desperate need of help in finding resolution. She would frequently have to kick me out of our sessions, saying "You have to leave now" or "You have to give me money now.". I would stumble out onto the street and wander through the rest of my day, trying to make sense of any of it.

I had started going to see her as a very confused, recently divorced 28-year-old, accused of emotionally abusing his ex-wife over the course of a six-year relationship. Such disruption and accusation in my life destroyed my self-confidence and left me as a crumpled, emotional mess. I didn't want to hurt people, of course. And I was frankly pretty lost as to how the situation had spiraled so badly out of control.

My ex had sent me a letter, which turned out to be our last communication. The recurring themes in it were about me failing to understand or hear her and my lack of understanding or respect for the importance of "little things." She was trying to tell me that I was missing—and thus violating—her boundaries. This theme continued to ring true throughout my therapy sessions.

I had initially approached my then-therapist to help me get a handle on my problems and keep them under control. Most of the reading said that an abusive personality should never be trusted and effort should be spent on healing survivors and I should be regarded as hopeless and a waste of time, given this diagnosis. This was highly troubling so I sought professional help. I had been in therapy before. I had even been in couple's therapy with my ex where she was just constantly frustrated with me. But this time felt different. My ex had demanded in her letter that I resolve issues stemming from my abusive upbringing through feminist counseling. It was more than reasonable but utterly terrifying to revisit my childhood in intensive therapy. During the first two months of our sessions, my therapist tried and tried to get a rise out of me and evaluated how responsible I felt about my own actions. She concluded that I took responsibility for my actions and didn't point blame on other people for things I had done. She felt that I did not exhibit traits of an abusive personality but that did not mean that our relationship was not abusive. I, thinking in terms of things in ones and zeroes, could not understand what any of this meant, and it just confused me more.

I remember telling my therapist about the physical violence, intimidation, and conditional love around my growing up, forever misapplied but causing me to try to stay in the good graces of my family through endless tumult. Eventually, at the end of one of our sessions, seemingly by chance, I mentioned that I could not ever see emotions by looking into people's faces. She explained to me that newborn babies can understand emotion and communication through nonverbal expression. My therapist seemed shocked, told me that it might indicate Asperger's, that we'd revisit it next time, and kicked me out as I wondered why this had never come up before at any point in the past thirty years.

On the way home I realized that people probably had explained this to me—and likely many times—just not in the singular ways that I could understand. As upsetting as all of these compounding realizations were in the short term, it was far more edifying. For relating to other people beyond surface interactions. Many times I'd watch people exit my life without explanation, at least not one that I understood. They wanted me to pick up on "signs," or as far as I was concerned, it felt like they wanted me to be psychic.

This realization quickly took over my therapy sessions. For the next six months I was pretty lost. What did it mean? How did society work? Would ever regain my confidence? Should I just move to a desert island? As a result of my lack of confidence, was clumsily trying to please everyone around me but was instead continually misstepping and creating more hurt and conflict. A life of solitude seemed like the safest way to proceed. Life just felt like an ongoing downward spiral. In a world of neurotypical people being framed as "normal," it seemed best for me to disengage and cause less harm.

About the time I gave up on finding a happy and harmonious relationship, I met my current partner. She was aware of the dramas in my life and accepted me anyway, having much more understanding of the nuances of situations like these than other people that was accustomed to. She was caring, listened closely and was supportive of me, but still pushed me to do better all the time and not just accept where I was at. She pushed me to be attentive and caring as best as was able to the people around me.

For me at that time, Asperger's meant that understood everything very literally and even now have a hard time understanding nuances and jokes because of it. I feel things deeply and intensely and have a hard time showing empathy with others because I have a hard time understanding emotion that aren't my own. (If I can relate someone's emotion to my own, I felt very deeply for them, but it s often difficult to get to that point). I used to need to hear something said out loud in plain language to understand it. Boundaries are rarely expressed in plain anguage. And perhaps therein lies the problem.

My therapist believes that very poor and ncompatible communication habits partnered with missed boundaries can create a lot of hurt, and those patterns and habits repeated daily could result in the same effects of relationship **emotional abuse**—to make it feel like a power struggle and to deeply impact the self-esteem of both parties.

In hindsight, I can recognize my ex reacting to feeling uncomfortable and the dynamics she was experiencing. She became physically violent towards me at times, everything became a tense negotiation she began dating other people while we were married and would "punish" me when I didn't behave or communicate in the ways that she wanted. It was painful and scary but it's now clear that from what she was experiencing, she was trying to get power back n the relationship. From what I gather, it seems that she felt expected or even obligated to go along with my decisions and that reacting in these ways, it felt like a reclamation of sorts. In one case, when my bicycle got stolen from my studio, she saw it locked up on the street and rather than trying to get it returned to me,

she simply took a photo and emailed it to me. Lack of communication and lack of understanding led her to feel as if she had been living under my rules and had to regain control, although I remained oblivious to this dynamic.

A real example of this kind of dynamic is a neurotypical person who tells their Asperger's partner, "Don't let that man set foot on our property" so the partner with Asperger's lays out boards for the visitor to walk on. With Asperger's, this is following orders to respect a partner's requests but to most neurotypical people it's highly manipulative and doing what one wants in spite of a request. And the big problem is that even with Asperger's, a person often has to co-exist with the rest of the world.

These revelations motivated me to understand my own predicament and see the situation outside the scope of a failed relationship that was likely doomed regardless. I could see the communication problems that I had been responsible for and it was time to get my life under control. I spent a lot of my time reading and researching. I found that there are typically two kinds of people who have relationships with A.S. individuals—other people with A.S. and neurotypicals with bad boundaries. The former tend to resemble typical relationships on the inside, though habits tend to appear strange from the outside. The latter tend to be highly dysfunctional and the neurotypical person tends to have their boundaries violated over and over by their A.S. date who has no idea that this is going on until everyone's patience is so exhausted that the relationship explodes into a bitter mess.

My comprehension of the situation became easier when I realized that both of my parents likely had Asperger's. They were born in the 1940s and 50s and were never diagnosed.

This was a very helpful piece of the puzzle as it explained how communication could devolve to such a degree that two different people in the same place were experiencing two very different things. At first I took the position that it was the responsibility of others to accommodate my neurology. But this, a privileged position that only adds further strain onto others, wasn't going to work. Further, men are raised and socialized to expect conformity and entitlement to our way of being and we have a responsibility to overcome that as much as we can. I slowly realized that this attitude put more strain on the underprivileged people in society who were constantly being told that it was their responsibility to accommodate the needs and wants of others and that there would be negative consequences for doing otherwise. Worst of all, this rationale left me not responsible for my own behavior, which is never acceptable.

My comprehension of the situation became easier when I realized that both of my parents likely had Asperger's. They were born in the 1940s and 50s and were never diagnosed.

For most of my life, I had found my mom to be very hard to deal with. She could almost never see my point of view, and it felt like she very much had to get her way, even though she likely did not see it that way. But this breakthrough made it much easier to see what had likely been going on. She was saying how she felt and not hearing how I felt.

So I came around to a better, more moderated solution. If someone denied my experience of having Asperger's, I would cease allowing them into my life. I would not share this detail about myself until I felt safe and comfortable and we had some emotional history and proximity. Opening up to these people was a risk, after all. Admittedly, for the people who had known me for much longer it was hard for them to combine it into the fabric of things that created my personality and character. Many people said that they were "not surprised" but some people stridently denied it, often based on limited knowledge of A.S. or knowing someone who was a much more severe case and much more limited. If they had known me in my pre-teen years, I think they would have no doubts about it.

I can't go back and resolve a lifetime of confusing and hurtful interactions and relationships but I was still in touch with most of the people I'd had serious relationships with, so I let each of them know, one by one, thinking that it might provide them with good closure of what was likely a confusing and difficult situation. I accepted that even though I was neurologically different than most people, I still had the responsibility of being respectful, loving, and careful in my behavior and being accountable when I hurt someone.

Instead of a batterer program for abusers, I began cognitive-behavioral therapy, a program designed to teach A.S. people how to interact with neurotypicals and recognize boundaries. I am an adult who is responsible for his own behavior, understanding it, and making changes to not negatively impact others. And with that, I've done my best. I've been retrained how to socialize healthfully and understand others' subtle communications and when someone might be expressing a boundary, as well as upholding clear and enforceable boundaries of my own.

Six years later, I've never been happier and have carved out a wonderful life by respecting other people's boundaries and defining my own. No amount of cognitive re-training can make me neurotypical, and I still make mistakes and do or say things that come across as callous, but I feel like it's been reduced by 95% and I found a balance that isn't totally crippling to my functionality. I identified three needs that must be met for me to be in a relationship and I continue to follow them: I need to be trusted, supported, and respected. I've found that when any of these elements are missing, there is a quick, downward spiral that seemingly can't be recovered from. It's not always easy, of course, but my new blood pact with the world already lead to restored confidence, stronger socialization, and even a new and healthy relationship.

I wish I'd had more time to discuss A.S. with the kid on the bus and, most importantly, tell him that it doesn't have to be a disability if he doesn't let it be one. It can be a superpower instead if you learn how to harness it correctly. And even people who don't live with A.S. can learn about boundaries and the need to respect others from its cartoonishly overstated examples.

BOUNDARIES: CROSSING THE LINE

Figuratively speaking, there are two ways to cross a line. One way is healthy, the other destructive. Sometimes we think of crossing boundaries as overcoming our own fears. After processing all of the regret and resentment that I had felt in my life, I knew that I was ready for a new beginning. In these moments of growth, it's natural to want to try something new, and we may discover that changing our own boundaries results in positive change. We may try something new that results in positive change.

The negative form of crossing the line means causing emotional damage by disregarding another person's boundaries. The individual may be a lover, a friend, or a stranger. The act may be physical, sexual, emotional or all of the above. Whether intentional or unintentional, if you've crossed someone else's line, you've hurt them.

You can cross divides in great ways when you are empowered and respecting the limits of those around you. But you should not use your own sexual or social liberation to pressure another person into a compromising situation. It's important to recognize this distinction. You always have the right to change and develop as an individual. Cross all the lines you want, as long as you understand that you cannot force others to join you. If you use your personal choices as justification for crossing someone else's boundaries, conflict will arise and you will risk hurting another person.

Examine your boundaries to see if they are compatible with the people around you. All relationships and people are different. A boundary may develop in a new experience or reappear from an old trauma. Disagreements in boundaries are expected when you interact with other people extensively, yet the results of arguments vary greatly. Ignoring a person's boundaries is emotionally hurtful, and sometimes crossing the line can become a physically violent act. Conflict in itself does not have to be dysfunctional, but all abusive interactions have at least one commonality—they all involve violating personal boundaries. The stories below describe real scenarios between couples when a disagreement about boundaries escalated to emotional, sexual, and/ or physical abuse.

Examples of Crossed Boundaries

1. Verbal and Emotional Abuse

Josh and Kim were high school sweethearts who bonded over their distaste for mainstream music. They mimicked a quirky chick flick in their attitude towards love, seeing alternative interests and rebelliousness as a reason to be together forever. Though Kim sometimes felt that Josh (being two years younger than her) was immature, they continued their relationship after high school.

Shortly after Josh's high school graduation, Kim's family home burned down in a wildfire, leaving Kim devastated and lost. All emotional support felt futile in the wake of the tragedy. Kim wanted Josh to participate more in her life, though he did not have the right tools to help her heal. Feeling that Josh did not want to help her, Kim lashed out at Josh's insecurities. He had barely graduated from high school and Kim told Josh repeatedly that she had little faith in his ability to excel in his classes. She emphasized her greater achievement in school and belittled Josh for taking lower level classes. By the time the sweethearts broke up, Josh felt extremely insecure about his intellectual ability and Kim felt abandoned, which carried into their future relationships.

Conflicts: Maturity, Support, Education

The emotional boundaries crossed by Kim may seem small compared to some abusive relationships, but they had lasting effects on Josh's self-esteem. On the other hand, Kim did not trust Josh after he had neglected to assist after the trauma. Because both partners were unable to recognize Josh's limits in helping Kim and did not recognize how outside counseling could have helped after Kim's trauma, the relationship became emotionally abusive at times.

Recognize when a partner needs more help than you can provide. Discuss outside resources of support for those experiencing a trauma. Without help, people may begin to lash out in unhealthy ways. Criticizing someone's intelligence can be an especially sensitive subject for those who have trouble in traditional learning environments. Everyone learns differently, so education and test scores do not accurately measure a person's ability. Emotionally injuring a person with insults could inhibit them from trusting future partners and developing their individual talents.

2. Sexual and Emotional Abuse

Megan and Nick dreamed of forming a traditional family together. They imagined Megan staying at home with their future children, while Nick worked full-time to financially support the family. Although Megan and Nick struggled with differences in their sex drives, their life plans seemed to be a perfect match.

Shortly before their wedding day, however, Megan began a new job that required extensive traveling. She enjoyed meeting new people in her position and sometimes felt attracted to other men, who were understanding of her changing plans. Nick felt that they both still had marital obligations to fulfill, including sex and starting a family. As a result, Nick crossed Megan's sexual boundaries by often pressuring her to have sex with him. After being sexually assaulted and recognizing that Nick continually crossed her boundaries, Megan decided to end the relationship.

Conflicts: Change in Mutual Plans, Sex Life

Commitment is an important part of any marriage, but often commitment is manipulated to enforce control over one another. In the case of Megan and Nick, Nick believed that their marriage required a commitment to structured plans and a certain amount of sex. But commitment within relationships, whether marriage or not, should represent a promise to respect one another. Megan made the right decision in ending the relationship, however, the violations inflicted on her still troubled her deeply. Nick could have prevented the emotional and sexual abuse he inflicted by respecting boundaries. If he had, the couple may have ended their relationship before it became abusive.

No one is ever obligated to partake in a sexual act, regardless of any preexisting relationship, contract, or agreement. If you find that you are in a relationship with someone whose **sex drive** is incompatible with your own, you have a right to leave the relationship. You do not have a right to sexually assault them.

3. Physical and Emotional Abuse

Marie was not interested in a romantic relationship; however, Ben, a man she had recently met, hoped to form a committed partnership with her. He doted on her and aggressively expressed his feelings. After a couple weeks of questioning Ben's romantic advances, Marie agreed to a casual relationship and was beginning to like him more. Still, some instances of unreciprocated affection angered Ben. They fought regularly about emotional support and Ben often felt that Marie wasn't attentive to his needs.

Several months into the relationship, Ben wanted to experience a threesome and expressed this desire to Marie. Marie was also interested in dating women, so they hoped to meet someone who would be a good match for both of them. Marie created an online dating profile and met a woman named Heather.

As Marie became closer to Heather, Ben questioned Marie's feelings for him again. Violating Marie's privacy, he searched through her email and text messages. In addition, Ben attempted to restrict Marie's communication with others. Fearing that Marie wasn't attracted to him and attempting to maintain control over her, Ben told Marie that she could no longer speak to Heather. From this point on, he insisted on being present anytime she met with friends and became more controlling of her physical movements. He had hit her arm once before in an attempt to keep her from leaving his apartment, and now his frustrations led to him physically attacking her multiple times.

As their friends began to notice Marie's bruises, the couple isolated themselves further, discontinuing contact with anyone who attempted to direct them towards domestic violence resources. Marie attempted to leave several times, but feared for her safety and felt emotionally tied to Ben. Their emotional dynamics of control had escalated into a physically abusive relationship.

Conflict: Distrust of Partner's Feelings, Control Issues

In some ways, Marie and Ben appeared compatible. They both had similar sexual boundaries and they seemed to be interested in becoming sexually involved with Heather together. From the very beginning of the relationship, however, Ben attempted to control Marie's actions. Likely due to insecurity, Ben felt that Marie was neglecting him anytime her actions didn't correspond with his wants.

Some people are able to have multiple partners and maintain healthy relationships. In these cases, it's crucial that everyone involved is aware and respectful of each other's boundaries. Knowing and respecting what your **partner** wants and doesn't want is the first step for forming trust in any relationship. If personal limits are either not expressed or ignored by a partner, the misunderstanding will lead to emotional pain and can cause violent abuse.

When a person intentionally hits their lover, it is clear that the relationship is abusive. The obvious intention to hurt another person makes it easier to define physical violence as abuse. It should be equally as obvious that abuse is occurring when we talk about sexual assault in relationships. But because of socialization into prescribed roles, described in previous chapters, sexual assault sometimes appears to be unclear. Sex may seem to be an obligation in a romantic relationship. This view of sex in relationships leads to some people pressuring their partners to have sex. Intentional abuse also extends to emotional violations that are being used to physically and/or sexually control another person. Emotional violations quickly become abuse when they are used to justify physical and sexual violence. When a person is forcing someone to do anything physically, no matter the means, we should recognize that they are crossing **universal boundaries.**

On the other hand, abusive behaviors fall into a gray area when interactions relate to an individual's **personal boundaries.** Verbal interactions, such as belittling a person, can cause great amounts of emotional damage, but it's difficult to discern whether or not the damage was intentional. If a partner attacks their partner's insecurities, they are generally intentionally hurting their partner. For instance, in the case of Josh and Kim, Kim's awareness of his intellectual insecurity made the interaction abusive. If different conditions had existed for the couple, a respectful discussion about school would not have resulted in emotional damage. **Triggers** are often a way to discover personal emotional boundaries. For instance, certain sexual positions trigger negative emotional responses for me. I am aware that I have emotional limits when it comes to sex due to past experiences. These sexual positions, however, would not have the same emotional effects for other people. Personal boundaries will always vary from one relationship to another.

In cases of **personal violations**, many times the solution is to ask questions. Ask yourself, ask your partner, ask your friends. Questions are as important as answers. Questions can help to steer respectful discussions in the right direction. If you do not know what your partner's boundaries are, it can be difficult

to keep yourself from crossing the line. Likewise, if your partner isn't aware of your boundaries, you may feel violated after certain interactions. To begin the process of finding boundaries and understanding what causes emotional damage, it can help to describe previous experiences that made you feel uncomfortable.

Because crossing the line creates distrust and resentment, respecting each other's boundaries is crucial for the survival of any healthy relationship. Whether the damage seems big or small, denying someone's boundaries means denying them control over their own life.

There will always be differences in how we perceive relationships, which is why conflict occurs often in intimate interactions. Discussing the conflict in a respectful manner, however, determines whether or not a relationship becomes dysfunctional. In the three relationships described in this chapter, at least one person crossed a partner's boundary after conflict developed. All of the instances weakened trust within the relationship and caused further harm.

If you aren't willing to respect your partner's boundaries or vice versa, then it is time to consider other options, such as counseling, ending the relationship, exploring new relationships, or all of the above. You have the right to desire a certain kind of sex, love, or partnership, but you don't have a right to hurt others by forcing them to conform to your ideals.

Questions to ask as soon as possible:

☐   What past interactions have made you feel uneasy, violated, and/or misunderstood?

☐   Are there certain things (e.g. images, sexual positions, graphic stories, etc.) that make you feel uncomfortable? What triggers the same feelings that you experienced during the negative interaction(s)?

Questions to ask during and/or after a conflict:

☐   What is the conflict? Isolate what you and your partner(s) disagree on. What are some options for resolving the conflict?

☐   Can you find a solution without crossing one another's boundaries? Are you willing to respect your partner's boundaries?

If you or a partner have ignored a boundary in the relationship, what boundary was it? How did it affect you and your partner(s)? How will you repair the negative effects of the conflict? Do you need to utilize the help of outside resources?

AN UPDATE FROM A CO-ADVENTURER

by Robert.

Hello again! It has been a long time since I first started writing "Maroon Menemy and Me." Let me quickly update you, kind readers, about my life since you've last read from me.

Alas, I have experienced my first heartbreak this summer. I gave myself entirely to a man, whom we shall call "S", but there was a restlessness, a consternation in his eye that my love only exacerbated. Noticing how flighty he was, I tried melting into his arms, but failed. Then, I let him grip me so hard and close against his breast, thinking maybe he'd melt into me, but there was nothing I could do to soothe his unrest. Foreseeing his abandonment, and preferring to be mauled by a herd of wild zebras rather than waste away in the half-life of being ignored as my Maroon Menemy had done, I induced him to break up our proto-relationship.

I lust now for a future of freedom and empowerment away from my parents' suffocating presence. My graduation from UCSD, job security, and a burgeoning sense of what I wish to do in graduate school, strengthen me; otherwise, I give into the crippling depressive bouts that hit me when I feel their damaging vibes desiccate my enjoyment for life. As an adaptive method to survive this unpleasantly long transition that I must still travail, I am perpetually on guard when around my parents, ever mindful that establishing and maintaining my boundaries is the only way I can preserve my pride, dignity, and self-respect around these people who have irretrievably lost my trust. Currently, I am defining my boundaries from my parents, and become very anxious when I do not know how to defend a trespassed boundary, especially when it is of a very vulnerable nature.

For me, the healthy boundaries that contain my sexual longings are not difficult to locate and discuss. However, my parents socialized into me their attitudes against male-male sex at an emotional level. Thankfully, they at least did not do so at an intellectual level. These past two years, it took me longer than I would have liked to debunk my fear of anal sex. In my mind and in my writing, men continued being an object of arduous longing; nonetheless, my dad's implicit condemnation of my sexuality as violent and perverse would interrupt my plans to bring these desires into reality. During one of my emotional, self-destructive attempts at convincing him that I exist and wished to fearlessly express my affection for men someday, he sarcastically asked me,

"What? Are you going to rape somebody?"

Ever since he spat that abhorrent question out of his mouth, I feel the generations of hate and ignorance that surround him every second I have to be around him. I would have but pitied him had his offense not affected me psychologically as it did. Perhaps the only thing more wounding was my mother pleading me to understand him. Reacting to this kind of **emotional abuse**, I would momentarily become filled with irrational panic and guilt. Perhaps he phrase "internalized homophobia" comes to you mind, but what I experienced was much more sinister. Since I had thankfully rid myself of it long ago, and now only accepted but embraced my homosexiness, what internalized this time was the message that I was a sexual threat to men, not that male-male sex was wrong. Had my dad merely spoken ill of the latter, I would have blocked it out, but he superimposed this distorted image of me-as-potential-rapist. My father trespassed my boundary; he worsened the already antagonistic relationship I had with myself and made me doubt the positive feelings I wish(ed) to share with men; even worse, he transposed to me an irrational fear of rape.

I ended up creating a boundary against my own desires. I was willing to perform anal sex on a man, knowing that I would do so consensually, and would rationalize my non-desire for its reception by saying it was simply not something I wanted to do, citing the preferences of other people who actually are comfortable within these parameters. My investment in consent became over-determined, as if I had some wrong for which I needed to compensate. Thinking about consent became less about increasing erotic satisfaction by knowing that one's partner is to be trusted, and more about conjuring up ways to escape from dangerous situations. The latter is most definitely a life-preserving reflection, but I would ruminate about them in such a way that I would feel afraid of men. Ironically, I blindly and numbly pursued activity with a dangerous man, almost as if I wanted to punish myself for the imaginary crime of which my father judged me.

Since then, I have become less self-destructive thanks to therapy undoing a lot of this imaginary guilt. By the time I met S, I was at a very peaceful place with my sexuality, reclaiming my naïveté for men that had been denied to me for so long. I felt young and clean again. I was ready to have a respectful, consensual man inside of me. I got precisely this, and more. I was loved; I knew it when he told me, "Yes, hold my hand, baby, I've got you."

The utter lack of parental support I experienced when, in a moment of grief, I told my mom of S's abandonment caused me to have a very empowering epiphany concerning sexuality. Recalling this book's theme of threes, I had always told myself, "As long as any erotic activities you do with yourself and others are safe, consensual, and legal, all is good." Now, however, I would add "dignified" to this list. Having had the strength to stomach my mother bashing gay men while I was seeking comfort from a break-up made me realize the infinite well of endurance I have had inside of me all along. Not only did I realize that she could no longer be privy to this area of my life, but I realized that my need to be respected trumped my feelings of domestic loneliness. With confidence, I have set an iron boundary between my parents and my amorous concerns with men. This decision has made me a lot more calculating and emotionally intelligent.

If there is anything I would have the readers of *Consensuality* hear from me, it is that our affections are sacred components of our human forms. A lot more important than the timing or enumeration of their consensual recipients is the level of dignity we retain as they receive them. Don't torture yourselves about setting your ideal goal for monogamy or polyamory in stone as I catch myself trying to do on a daily basis. It is definitely mature to communicate these preferences with your partner(s) as they develop, but the road to discovering them will likely include participating in their alternatives. Although we are all prone to err, and allow people to disregard our boundaries or assume we have them where we would rather prefer closeness; where we would prefer to be cuddled and kissed, a healthy dosage of self-compassion will remind you that no one has the right, ability, or hope to tarnish or limit the joys your warm bodies will have throughout the course of your sexy lives.

Evaluating Your Relationship(s)

Now you've seen my subjective reality and various complications.

So what can you do?

There are many things that can complicate the ways we create consent and respect. Relationships are a complex interaction of social factors and emotional influences. But what keeps consent going even after you have navigated through gender, feminism, and sexual boundaries? What comes next?! The three exercises in this chapter will become your personal creations. Although I've included my own experiences throughout the book, *Consensuality* is your opportunity to invent your own personal narrative towards healthy relationships.

The process of creating positive forms of companionship never ends, so it's crucial to ensure that we maintain healthy habits in all of our interactions. Follow the questions throughout the chapter to also discover the healthy parts of your relationships. Use all of the thoughts, feelings, and ideas, that you've explored in *Consensuality* to envision, create, and maintain respect in your relationships.

How do you see yourself, in relation to and separate from others' opinions? What is your view of gender, sexuality, and relationships?

1. Recognize your perspective. Explore what you need from yourself and others.

What I wanted ten years ago would sound like it came straight out of a cheesy romance novel: tall, dark, and handsome. I was focused on finding the perfect man. But I was later disappointed when many men, who appeared to be great and handsome, had antiquated views of dating and sex. I had to return to the basics and reevaluate what I needed for myself. I wanted to explore how my feminist perspective would fit into the world.

While I can only speak for myself, I want to learn from others' perspectives. As a white, heterosexual woman, I understand that others have an equal right to express their own form of feminism and my perspective often assumes privilege in the feminist narrative. One of the many things I want to recognize for myself is how this privilege of race and sexual orientation shapes my words and actions. I want to understand as much as possible how my privilege affects others, so that I can listen and change my role in society.

I also want to challenge the disadvantages imposed on me because of my gender. Despite societal progress, I still feel limits on my emotions, my appearance, and my physical movement as a woman. I want to travel freely, without fear of physical harm. I want to feel confident within my relationships, instead of supporting the idealized passivity of females. I want to feel free to express what I want during sexual interactions. Some of these wants currently seem out of reach on a societal level, but I am happy that I'm working towards creating them within my personal relationships.

> At this point, you're exploring your perspective and what you want. If you currently have a partner, are they willing to understand your perspective?

When you are sharing your wants and needs in a relationship, clearly talk about how perspective shapes your values. In addition, encourage your partner(s) to do the same. If you disregard your partners' perspective or vice versa, it will become difficult to feel comfortable around one another. Be aware of how dismissing a person's perspective can make it difficult to express consent, and avoid unhealthy patterns by ending interactions before they become abusive.

2. What can you learn from your mistakes?

Forming respectful relationships includes expressing your values to others, but it is important to examine our

> What actions challenge your ability to form healthy relationships? How do you respond to and own your mistakes?

actions along the way. Even after talking about gender and sexuality with the people in my life, I still encoun-

tered bumps in the road, and sometimes my actions didn't coincide with my beliefs.

I once cheated on a partner while he was out of town for a couple weeks. At the beginning of his trip, we spoke on the phone and I expressed concerns about our relationship. Our conversations felt distant through the phone. I was having a hard time connecting with him, literally and emotionally, and was feeling increasingly drawn to someone who had been a romantic influence in my life on and off over the past year. After discovering how important the other person was to me, we chose to express our attraction to each other by having sex.

When it was time for my partner to return, I rationalized to myself that I had warned him by expressing how I felt distant, but I had never directly addressed my attraction to another person. I realized that my words had not coincided with my actions, so I did my best to reestablish open communication between us. My best, in that moment, wasn't all that great. I stood there for ten minutes, trying to squeak out a sound before blurting out, "I cheated on you." That moment wouldn't win any awards for communication, but it was better than hiding. The conversation commenced.

Did you use the best tool for communication? Are you being completely honest? If not, how do you create open communication as the conversation continues?

I knew I loved him, but I knew that it was difficult for me to be monogamous and that I had

108

serious feelings for someone else. We would have had a better chance of making it if I had asked for an open relationship in the beginning. From that point on, I needed to express verbally and physically how I wanted a different kind of relationship.

Maybe it wasn't the most socially acceptable way to handle the situation, but I couldn't claim that we would be exclusive if he forgave me. I couldn't erase how I hurt him and I couldn't change my feelings to end my relationship with the other person. He deserved the truth so he could move forward and make a decision after knowing the whole story.

We attempted to continue our relationship, but for understandable reasons, he guarded his feelings. I never got to hear his full perspective on the situation. He was generally very quiet around me and preferred to talk about lighter subjects. I could only see from his isolation that I had emotionally hurt him.

I felt guilty, and guilt from my actions was different from the regret I felt when I did nothing. I had to go through it, so I tried to go through it with the least amount of casualties, the least amount of hurt. I tried to continue the conversation, while understanding that he deserved the right to space and time away from me.

Hurting my previous partner led to me communicating with my current partner when I have feelings for other people. I've become more conscious during physical encounters with my partner, as well as talking about them, and how they reflect our beliefs

in a healthy relationship. It wasn't easy to start a new relationship with the admittance that we hurt another person and the possibility of other partners in the future, but being honest was worth the complications.

> **3. Finally, combine it all, romance, health and happiness. Write a love note on how you're committed to creating a healthy relationship(s).**

A Different Kind of Love Note

A love note can feel like something is being stolen away each time you put a word on the page. It can feel as if there is the risk of losing something. There are reasons to be fearful, but there are also ways of improving how we love. My love stories have been spouted out of me, as gossip, as threats, as ramblings, but the following tale is a permanent record of my true love, a love that means respect for myself and others.

I often used the word "crazy" in matters of love. It was thrown around even before my partner and I could obtain a mutual sense of feelings about our relationship. From the beginning, I had a "crazy" attraction to my partner. I didn't know what to expect when we started dating, but I knew from experiences in past relationships that I didn't want to be with someone who would restrict me. I had to fall completely for us as partners, not just for him. I had to know that we wouldn't control each other through our interactions together, whether that was conscious on his part or just the way it played out in practice.

We can't always expect others to understand us innately, so we need ways to communicate our boundaries, needs, and wants in a way that doesn't confuse or misdirect our partner.

DIVULGE

"When you do _____,
it makes me feel _____."

"_____ is something
I like to do/share/take part in."

LET IT OUT

Now come up with some
questions of your own!

_____
_____
_____
_____
_____
_____

I thought it would be pleasant to be with someone nice. I was ready to work towards respecting each other in a mutually consenting relationship. What I didn't know was that looking for positive and free communication with another person could create an intense love. While looking for a different kind of love, I initially discovered that a seemingly shy boy could be a magnificent and somewhat scary creature. He had glimpses of freedom. His ten toes were dotted with ink to spell out his spontaneity. He moved uncontrollably to New Order at the dance parties that he enjoys so much. I had been controlled for so long that it drove me "crazy" how much fun he and I were able to have together.

How have you expressed love in the past, in positive or negative ways? Why did you express your love in this way?

Initially, all I could feel was "crazy," yet we hadn't crossed a boundary or restricted one another. We felt incredibly free in the relationship. The thing I realize now is that it's difficult to express, feel, and sustain freedom. Communication can deteriorate into awkward and painful misunderstandings when partners are holding back or just poorly matched, but communication turned into freedom when we started expressing ourselves respectfully. It took time to learn how to completely show ourselves and understand each other. In fact, we needed to take time away from each other along the way.

My partner and I were evolving into more honest and open people, but we hadn't examined how this would affect our relationship. We were free the night we decided to be partners while dancing at a party. We were free the first time we had sex when we weren't afraid to ask all of the questions on our mind.

We were free at my sister's wedding when we forgot how much we hate marriage and remembered how much we love each other. We had many fun moments, where we forgot about the issues from our pasts, but we rarely reflected on how our past experiences were leading to our connection with one another.

Recently, we had an open conversation about a subject that I had never felt comfortable discussing. I had found an article stating that the best rape prevention was for college women to stop getting drunk. It was an emotional trigger because I have experienced non-consensual sex multiple times under the influence of alcohol. Articles that unfairly blamed and stereotyped female victims made me afraid to call what happened to me sexual assault.

> If you're feeling "crazy" in a current relationship, take a moment to step back and examine why. Have either of you violated a personal boundary? Do you feel uncomfortable with some of your partner's actions? If you answer yes, stop here and discuss these boundaries. Understand how this relationship is challenging your personal needs.

A few nights prior, our friends had also talked about an instance when a woman had sexually assaulted my partner years before we met. My partner had previously had sex with the woman and regretted it. When he saw her a second time, he asked his friends to ensure that he was not left alone with her. After an outing to a park and many drinks, they all returned to a friend's house, but the woman told my partner that he should stay in the car. The woman then got on top of my partner and had sex with him, despite him telling her to stop multiple times. As our friends recounted the story, they laughed. They wrote it off as a drunken mistake. I felt bad that his traumatic experience had been turned into a joke. I wanted him to know that I would understand if he wanted to talk about what had happened to him.

> *If you or your partner haven't crossed any boundaries but are still experiencing conflict, look further into your compatibility with your partner. Are your fun and crazy moments masking more serious issues? When things aren't going well, is your partner supportive of you and vice versa? Are they discouraging you from expressing your feelings, either intentionally or unintentionally? If so, talk to your partner about how their actions or words affect you.*

My partner and I had never thoroughly discussed the topic, but seeing that article made me realize that I want to be with someone who acknowledges that non-consensual sex, even if it is with a partner and/or under the influence of alcohol, is sexual assault and is not the fault of the victim. Talking about sexual assault was scary for both of us. I thought that he wasn't acknowledging our experiences with sexual assault, and he was worried that I was mad at him for not previously understanding what consent means.

Thankfully, all that was required for us to work through these fears was that we were both willing to respectfully communicate. We talked about our experiences and how they affected us. He wanted to know how I felt when we would have sex after a night of drinking. It had happened before, but felt consensual. We realized, however, that even if we usually felt like sex under the influence was fine between us, it was problematic to think that it would always be ok. What if there was a night in the future when one of us didn't want to have sex but felt pressured.

We ultimately decided that we wouldn't have sex when our judgment was impaired because sex is never worth the possibility of violating each other. Anytime we hurt one another or recognize the potential to hurt one another, we have an open discussion to resolve the issue together. We won't be able to foresee every risk, but it's liberating to know that we can talk about any topic and find a resolution that works for us. The discussion helped us understand what consent means to us.

To continue patterns of health like the experiences described in this chapter, it's important to share our perspectives and communicate with others. In the final pages of this book, consider the healthy

tools of communication that you currently use and will continue to use in your relationships.

Always ask questions; when you're considering relationships, when you're on a date, when you're kissing someone, and definitely when you're having sex with someone. Check in with each other by asking simple questions, such as "how are you doing?," "does this feel good for you?," "are you comfortable with this?" And answer these questions respectfully with your honest emotions. Although some phrases and words can counteract our feelings, one phrase that I will never remove from my vocabulary is "I feel." When someone asks you a question or you need to express a reason for conflict, don't be afraid to say "I feel..."

> *If you and your partner find a healthy resolution to a conflict, make note of how you handled the situation. Continue to develop your pattern of health. If you generally do not find a way to resolve the conflict or if discussion causes more negative feelings, recognize the destructive patterns of the relationship and decide if this relationship is right for you.*

People are cautious when communicating about relationships because talking it out doesn't always work, but that doesn't have to be a bad thing. Sometimes communicating can also help us understand when we need to leave a dysfunctional relationship. We are taught that we will be saved by a knight in shining armor or that we will rescue a princess at the end of a story. If you aren't that knight or that princess—and make no mistake, most of us aren't—you'll feel forgotten until you realize that you can write your own alternative narratives. When it comes to love in companionship, each relationship is its own unique set of interactions.

The journey towards understanding consent opens up many options for how you can express your own version of *Consensuality* in your relationships. When you establish open lines of communication with another person, an intense and respectful bond develops that helps you feel comfortable with saying yes, no, or anything else that you feel in the moment. I wouldn't have been able to find respect for myself without the process of finding my *Consensuality*. It has helped me feel confident in our ability as people to create healthy, respectful relationships. I feel empowered by all of the voices that choose to represent consent in their relationships, and I refuse to say sorry for that!

If you're experiencing **immediate danger or fear** in your relationship, call for help. Call **Safe Horizon 800.621.HOPE** or the **National Domestic Violence Hotline 1-800-799-7233**

For further reading, check out:

Why Does He Do That?: Inside the Minds of Angry and Controlling Men by Lundy Bancroft

The Verbally Abusive Relationship: How to recognize it and how to respond by Patricia Evans

Stop Signs: Recognizing, Avoiding, and Escaping Abusive Relationships by Lynn Fairweather

Self Love

by Meme Pride

Thinking about the term "partner"; what does it mean to you? To me, it suggests another half, a person you can rely on and can trust to join you in life, in all activities. It embodies the ultimate form of trust and mutual respect; it is a term that comes with big shoes to fill. It took me a while to realize what this term means to me, and since acknowledging it I feel I make better decisions and think things through more thoroughly before giving my consent in a romantic or sexual situation.

I view my multiple friend groups, my various good friends, and select "best friends" as small pieces to ultimately form this greater picture of a "partner", each person supplying (and receiving) love and respect, and satisfying my various needs. Many times I have surveyed my past romantic relationships and realized that while they taught me a lot, I often was left feeling unsatisfied or unhappy with the experience. I, like many others who have invested themselves in another person romantically, have learned how it feels to be let down or undervalued. I also, like many other people, have settled for less than I deserve or allowed myself to be put in uncomfortable positions for the sake of pleasing a love interest, which I now see is only compromising myself.

I have screamed and bickered with men in parking lots, always left feeling irrational, upset, and more distant from them than ever; and each time after a situation like this, I would sit in my car and comfort myself. Through each low, I take a time out and survey myself. I can proudly say I have come to realize and embrace the fact that I am my best friend, my most capable healer; the relationship with myself is the happiest and healthiest I have known. I have taken the time to know myself, I have asked myself what I want, what I like, what I think, and how I feel about things. In knowing myself, and through channeling past bad relationship experiences to learn more about my needs, I have found it possible to have a loving, consensual, respectful relationship with *myself*. In this way, I make more informed decisions, I make fewer mistakes, I build happy relationships with people that I respect and love. I have gained enough self-respect to say no when I want to, and to recognize and remove the toxicities from my life. I am happy and stable, and more able to supply support to others who need it; no longer making time for people I know do not respect me in the way I deserve. I have found more free time to spend on my hobbies, myself, and people I love. The best kind of consent you can give is to say yes to yourself; say yes to self-respect, and to saying no (or yes!) in all situations you encounter.

Green Flags
by Rose Garden

I spent a few years looking for red flags. I was trying to figure out everything that was broken with my relationships and friendships. I read a lot of books and analyzed and critiqued the behavior of everyone around me, including—especially—my own actions and choices. I was no longer able to watch any movie or read any novel without feeling disgust and dismay at the gender power dynamics. I saw friends' and even strangers' relationships and interactions in a new, disconcerting light.

This intense period was necessary and helpful—but after a while I started to realize that I was only seeing the bad in everyone. I was setting better boundaries and making smarter life choices, but I also felt unhappy and angry every day. So I worked hard to shift my perspective again and try to see and strive for something better. With great effort I began to focus on good dynamics, healthy and equal relationships and friendships, my own strengths, fun and laughter. I cultivated an attitude of self-sufficiency and perspective in cases where nothing better could be helped, such as with my family.

In talking about green flags with some friends, here are a few that we had noticed in our own lives:

LOOK FOR THIS

- Listening to each other is the best sign of respect.
- You are able to share your feelings with each other non-judgmentally, even when it's hard.
- Relationship decisions made when sober tend to be more sustainable.
- You laugh at each others' jokes.
- When you tell them that something they are doing bothers you, they hear you and make changes as needed.
- You value their work, opinions, and what they're trying to accomplish in life.
- You don't necessarily have the same interests, but they are interested in what you are all about.

- You are each proven to be trustworthy with each other's problems, secrets, and concerns.
- If someone treats other people they are close to well, they'll treat you well. (And this also means—they are close to other people.)
- You're both able to recognize existing power dynamics, talk about them, and challenge them together.
- They respect your physical and emotional boundaries and reveal vulnerable information about themselves gradually over time.
- They are comfortable enough with themselves that they do not constantly seek attention from you or from others.
- They have emotionally moved on from previous relationships.
- You both are reliable and consistent with each other, follow through on plans, and respect each other's time.
- You each take responsibility for your life, your decisions, your feelings, and the consequences of their actions without blaming others.
- Their life isn't overrun with drinking or drugs, and if they partake, their personality does not significantly change and they remain in control of their decisions when they do.
- You can give each other constructive feedback without the other person getting defensive.

- They are able and willing to talk about their feelings from present and past times of their life.
- When you are talking about your relationship with friends, you hear yourself naturally talking about the positives.
- They remain close to you when you are experiencing hardship or dark times.
- You two are able and willing to reach compromises together because you recognize the value of your relationship above any disagreement.
- You feel comfortable because you authentically are yourself when you are together.

*　　　*　　　*

Of course, there is no relationship with only green flags (I've found that when I start thinking about someone or something as perfect, that's the biggest red flag that there is). But I've found that my most fulfilling relationships and friendships are based on the shared goal of mutual respect, fun, and creatively helping each other to have the best possible time in life.

Life and love are messy. Go forth and do them!

A GLOSSARY OF HOW

Agency
—the capacity of an individual to act independently and to make free choices without outside dictation

Cisgender
—an adjective that may describe you if your gender expression corresponds with the traits culturally associated with the sex assigned to you at birth

Consensuality
—the combination of universal boundaries and your personal boundaries, and how they are expressed, respected, and maintained within your relationships

Consent
—a voluntary verbal affirmation expressed while in a sober state-of-mind that you would like to engage in a specific act in that moment. True consent allows for a person to change their mind, even if the act has already begun

Emotional Abuse
—any damage done to a person's confidence, emotions, feelings, etc. It can often come in the form of ignoring your partner's needs, boundaries, or feelings

Gender
—the label, usually male or female, assigned to you at birth, based on genitalia and genetics

TERMS RELATE TO YOU!

Gender Expression

—how you express yourself throughout your life, using traits that are often associated with a culturally defined gender category

Partner

—someone with whom you are involved in an intimate relationship, where you understand each other's desires and respect one another's boundaries

Patriarchy

—a social system in which men hold the majority of leadership roles and exert disproportionate influence over societal values (i.e. male head of household)

Personal Boundaries

—physical, sexual, and emotional limits set within relationships to protect yourself and others

Personal Violation

—when you or another person feel disrespected because boundaries have been crossed or needs have been ignored

Physical Abuse

—when one person physically harms another person, often a result of repressed feelings and lack of communication

A GLOSSARY OF HOW

Privilege

—advantages given to you or others for possessing traits that are disproportionately valued globally or within a specific culture (e.g. white-privilege, male-privilege, straight-privilege)

Sexual Abuse

—anytime one's boundaries are crossed during or pertaining to sex. Within a relationship, sexual abuse may occur when you or your partner expects a certain amount of sex or believes that the other should have the same sex-drive

Sexual Assault

—a sexual act in which one or more people are coerced, threatened, or forced to engage in involuntary sex. As a legal term, sexual assault can vary from country to country, state to state, even community to community. For instance, California passed a "Yes means Yes" law in September 2014. The law requires for people participating to obtain affirmative consent from their partner(s) when engaging in sexual acts, but only applies to college students

Sex Drive

—how often you want to have sex, which can vary based on personal preferences, sexual attraction to another person, and your comfort level with another person

TERMS RELATE TO YOU!

Sexual Orientation

—labels, such as homosexual, heterosexual, and bisexual, based on who you find yourself sexually attracted to

They, them

—a gender-neutral plural pronoun, also used as a gender neutral singular pronoun in *Consensuality*

Transgender

—an adjective that may describe you if your gender expression differs from the traits culturally associated with the sex assigned to you at birth

Triggers

—words, images, experiences, or anything that causes extreme discomfort for you or another person, often associated with a previous trauma

Universal Boundaries

—limits on exerting physical and sexual control over another person, which should be globally recognized to protect the rights of all people (i.e. why murder is illegal)

Verbal Abuse

—often as damaging as physical abuse, it is a form of verbal attack that usually consists of triggering insults and hurtful words

SUBSCRIBE TO EVERYTHING WE PUBLISH!

Do you love what Microcosm publishes?

Do you want us to publish more great stuff?

Would you like to receive each new title as it's published?

Subscribe as a BFF to our new titles and we'll mail them all to you as they are released!

$10-30/mo, pay what you can afford. Include your t-shirt size and month/date of birthday for a possible surprise! Subscription begins the month after it is purchased.

microcosmpublishing.com/bff